What is Quantitative Longitudinal Data

'What is?' Research Methods series
Edited by Graham Crow

The 'What is?' series provides authoritative introductions to a range of research methods which are at the forefront of developments in the social sciences. Each volume sets out the key elements of the particular method and features examples of its application, offering a consistent structure across the whole series. Written in an accessible style by leading experts in the field, this series is an innovative pedagogical and research resource.

What are Community Studies?
Graham Crow

What is Diary Method?
Ruth Bartlett and Christine Milligan

What is Discourse Analysis?
Stephanie Taylor

What is Inclusive Research?
Melanie Nind

What is Narrative Research?
Corinne Squire, Mark Davis,
Cigdem Esin, Molly Andrews,
Barbara Harrison, Lars-Christer Hydén
and Margareta Hydén

What is Online Research?
Tristam Hooley, John Marriott and Jane Wellens

What is Qualitative Interviewing?
Rosalind Edwards and Janet Holland

What is Qualitative Research?
Martyn Hammersley

What are Qualitative Research Ethics?
Rose Wiles

What is Social Network Analysis?
John Scott

Forthcoming books:

What is Qualitative Longitudinal Research?
Bren Neale

What is Rhythmanalysis?
Dawn Lyon

What is

quantitative longitudinal data analysis?

Vernon Gayle and Paul Lambert

Bloomsbury Academic
An imprint of Bloomsbury Publishing Plc

B L O O M S B U R Y

LONDON · OXFORD · NEW YORK · NEW DELHI · SYDNEY

Bloomsbury Academic

An imprint of Bloomsbury Publishing Plc

50 Bedford Square	1385 Broadway
London	New York
WC1B 3DP	NY 10018
UK	USA

www.bloomsbury.com

BLOOMSBURY and the Diana logo are trademarks of Bloomsbury Publishing Plc

First published 2018

© Vernon Gayle and Paul Lambert, 2018

Vernon Gayle and Paul Lambert have asserted their right under the Copyright, Designs and Patents Act, 1988, to be identified as Authors of this work.

British Library Cataloguing-in-Publication Data
A catalogue record for this book is available from the British Library.

ISBN: HB: 978-1-4725-1539-1
PB: 978-1-4725-1540-7
ePDF: 978-1-4725-1542-1
ePub: 978-1-4725-1541-4

Library of Congress Cataloging-in-Publication Data
Names: Gayle, Vernon, author. | Lambert, Paul (Lecturer), author.
Title: What is quantitative longitudinal data analysis? / Vernon Gayle and Paul Lambert.
Description: London ; New York: Bloomsbury Academic, 2017. | Series: The 'What is?' research methods series; 11 | Includes bibliographical references and index.
Identifiers: LCCN 2017019301| ISBN 9781472515391 (hb) | ISBN 9781472515407 (pb)
Subjects: LCSH: Social sciences–Statistical methods. | Social sciences–Longitudinal studies. | Longitudinal method. Classification: LCC HA29 .G26 2017 | DDC 001.4/2–dc23 LC record available at https://lccn.loc.gov/2017019301

Cover design by Paul Burgess
Cover image © -strizh-/Shutterstock

Series: The 'What is?' Research Methods Series

Typeset by Deanta Global Publishing Services, Chennai, India
Printed and bound in Great Britain

To find out more about our authors and books visit www.bloomsbury.com. Here you will find extracts, author interviews, details of forthcoming events and the option to sign up for our newsletters.

Contents

List of figures

List of tables

Preface

There is now a wide portfolio of quantitative longitudinal data available to social science researchers. Many social science research questions can be adequately answered without longitudinal data; however, most research projects will benefit from the addition of longitudinal data analysis, and some research questions can only feasibly be answered using longitudinal data. Computers are now much faster and have larger storage capacities, and they are now far less expensive. Data analysis software is better developed and can analyse large and complex datasets more easily. The expansion of data resources and the improvement to computers and software have led to a manumission of social science research possibilities.

The subject of this book is quantitative longitudinal data analysis. It focuses on the data that are collected in large-scale social surveys, drawing particularly upon examples from the UK. The overall aim is to provide an introduction and an up-to-date overview of influential approaches to quantitative longitudinal data analysis in the social sciences.

We have been actively engaged in the analysis of large-scale survey datasets since the start of our academic careers as social scientists in the 1990s and we began delivering workshops and training activities on longitudinal data analysis in the early 2000s. We are forceful advocates for large-scale social science data resources. The orientation of the book is the result of many extended conversations, especially walking around Airthrey Loch and at half-time at Forthbank Stadium. The content has been greatly shaped by our experiences of delivering training sessions and teaching researchers, postgraduates and undergraduates. The examples that have been selected are the result of positive comments about their clarity and effectiveness. We have also received some brickbats over the years, and they have persuaded us to omit certain examples and topics.

We admire Joshua Angrist and Jörn-Steffen Pischke's book *Mostly Harmless Econometrics*, not only for its intellectual contribution but also because it introduces a diet of complicated, and possibly dry, topics in an engaging manner. We have attempted to emulate this style and to communicate directly with researchers who wish to learn more about quantitative longitudinal data analysis. The main body of the book tells the reader 'what is' longitudinal data analysis. The final chapter of the book is more practical and describes 'how to begin to do' longitudinal data analysis using the data analysis software package Stata. The syntax for undertaking analyses using Stata is interwoven throughout the book to help the reader to better understand how the software can be used for specific analyses. Students and participants on our courses have frequently reported that they have found this practice especially useful.

We envisage that readers will get the most benefit out of the book if they read it sequentially. It is, however, possible to dip in and out of the text. Some of the data analysis examples are best understood within the sequence that they have been arranged, but they can also be used as stand-alone examples. Organizing analyses within a systematic workflow is integral to the successful statistical analysis of social survey data, and it is especially important when working with large-scale longitudinal datasets. We advise all readers to consult Gayle and Lambert (2017), which provides detailed prescriptions on the social science data analysis workflow. We are fairly certain that it will help most researchers regardless of how much experience they have analysing social survey data.

Specialist data analysis techniques are required to analyse large-scale quantitative longitudinal datasets. These techniques can initially be perplexing; however, we hope to demonstrate that readers can make progress and rapidly acquire necessary skills. The analysis of quantitative longitudinal data will provide intellectual returns for the extra analytical efforts that are inevitably required.

Most of all we hope to convey our enthusiasm for analysing large-scale longitudinal social science data.

Good Luck.

Series editor's foreword

The idea behind this series is a simple one: to provide concise and accessible overviews of a range of frequently used research methods and of current issues in research methodology. Books in the series have been written by experts in their fields with a brief to write about their subject for a broad audience who are assumed to be interested but not necessarily to have any prior knowledge. The series is a natural development of presentations made in the 'What is?' strand at the Economic and Social Research Council Research Methods Festivals, which have proved popular both at the festivals themselves and subsequently as a resource on the website of the ESRC National Centre for Research Methods.

Methodological innovation is the order of the day, and the 'What is?' format allows researchers who are new to a field to gain an insight into its key features, while also providing a useful update on recent developments for people who have had some prior acquaintance with it. All readers should find it helpful to be taken through the discussion of key terms, the history of how the method or methodological issue has developed and the assessment of the strengths and possible weaknesses of the approach through an analysis of illustrative examples.

This eleventh book in the series is devoted to quantitative longitudinal data analysis. In it, Vernon Gayle and Paul Lambert take readers through a field of social science research that provides a uniquely powerful perspective on patterns of social change and continuity. Large-scale social surveys are undertaken on aspects of economics and social life ranging from employment to health, education to housing, household composition to political attitudes, leisure to religious identification and many other issues. When these surveys are conducted repeatedly (ideally at regular intervals as in the case of the UK Household Longitudinal Study) the results provide a wealth of information about the extent to which society is changing. They provide insights into social processes such as ageing, the growth of household diversity, rising levels of educational achievement, and social and geographical mobility. However, our knowledge of these social processes requires not simply the collection of data about all of these phenomena but also the analysis of those data. Data analysis is a key skill that allows social researchers to go beyond descriptive statistics about changing levels of owner occupation and renting in housing, or shifting patterns of attitudes to political issues, and to explore the nature of the underlying processes. It is one thing to establish that there is a connection between unemployment and ill health, which can readily be shown, but more sophisticated analysis is needed to determine whether the influential relationship runs from unemployment to ill health or ill health to unemployment. This example is one of many that the authors discuss in this book in order to demonstrate the power of longitudinal data analysis to enlighten us – academics, policymakers and lay readers alike – about how the social world is changing. Change may come about as a consequence of policy interventions, or it may be the unintended result of individual behaviour working itself through at the societal level. Unprecedented amounts of quantitative longitudinal data are now available, along with sophisticated analytical tools that previous generations of researchers could only have dreamt of. The authors of this book show the enormous potential of working in this field and encourage readers to learn the skills to take up this opportunity.

The books in this series cannot provide information about their subject matter down to a fine level of detail, but they will equip readers with a powerful sense of reasons why it deserves to be taken seriously and, it is hoped, with the enthusiasm to put that knowledge into practice.

Graham Crow

Acknowledgements

We would like to thank Graham Crow, the series editor, for approaching us and suggesting this project. We would also like to thank him for his patience and continued encouragement. Roxanne Connelly and Sarah Stopforth deserve a special mention for their insightful comments and for being available at very short notice to comment on draft chapters. Sarah also forensically reviewed the final version, for which we are extremely grateful. We would like to thank Hannah Buchanan-Smith, Chris Playford, Kevin Ralston, Audrey Thomas, Andrew Thompson and Malcolm Quon for their comments on draft chapters and their helpful suggestions. We would also like to thank Richard Davies and Damon Berridge, who in the past provided useful ideas on teaching longitudinal data analysis. We are grateful to our colleagues Robert Wright, David Bell, Paul Boyle, Robin Flowerdew and John Field for their inputs during various workshops and training events that we delivered during the 'two-thousands'. The work has greatly benefitted from comments and questions from numerous participants who have attended various workshops and training events that we have delivered.

We have been fortunate enough to be able to trial the material in this book within a Q-Step module on longitudinal data analysis and were heartened by the positive responses from the students.

Vernon Gayle would like to thank Heather Thompson and Stacey Rudkin-Johnstone at AQMeN for their tireless work and very good humour when organizing workshops. He would also like to thank his nephew Ben Buchanan-Smith, who encouraged him to buy a guitar and try to relearn a few tunes, which proved to be relaxing at various times over the last year. Vernon would also like to thank U.C. Berkeley for providing a pleasant and engaging environment in which to complete this book.

1 Introduction to quantitative longitudinal data

Tempus et maris aestus neminem expectant (Time and tide wait
   for no man)
The earliest known record is possibly from St. Marher, 1225

Introduction

The subject of this book is quantitative longitudinal data analysis, and
it focuses on data that are collected in large-scale social surveys. The
most universal definition of longitudinal social science data is any data
that have a temporal (i.e. time) dimension. A rudimentary distinction is
routinely made between cross-sectional designs, where data are collected
at only one point in time, and longitudinal designs, where information
is collected from the same units on multiple occasions. Temporal data
can be collected in cross-sectional designs, and it is mildly misleading to
assume that longitudinal analyses can never be undertaken with cross-
sectional data.

Longitudinal social science data are critical to understanding social
change over time. They are also critical to understanding social stability,
but this is often overlooked. The analysis of quantitative longitudinal data
has made a number of important intellectual contributions. Here are
three examples. First, the analysis of longitudinal data on British children
revealed a link between smoking during pregnancy and subsequent child
development (see Butler and Goldstein, 1973). Second, the Whitehall
Study revealed that inequalities in health were not limited to the health
consequences of poverty and demonstrated that occupational hierarchy
was intimately related to health and life chances (Marmot and Brunner,
2005; Marmot, 2004). Third, in the early 1990s much of the analyses of
income in Britain focused on poverty and social inequality. Inequality and
poverty rates then flattened off, and it appeared that there was little or no
change in the income distribution from one year to the next. The analysis

of longitudinal household data revealed that underneath the apparent stability there was a hidden flux. Household incomes fluctuated between one year and the next, and there was substantial turnover in the membership of the low-income population. This was well known in countries like the United States and Germany, which already had longitudinal household surveys. These new findings made a contribution to the understanding of poverty and to the development of new economic theory. They also influenced the Labour government's welfare reforms. The concept that household poverty is dynamic now influences the way living standards are measured and monitored in Britain (see Jenkins, 2000).

Many social science research questions can be adequately answered using cross-sectional data. Most social science research projects can be improved by incorporating suitable longitudinal data. Some social science research questions can only be sensibly answered using longitudinal data. The following chapter introduces concepts associated with analysing large-scale quantitative social science data and highlights the rich variety of data resources that are available to researchers. In this book we focus upon observational social survey designs, but most of the issues can be directly extended to other forms of data, for example administrative data or experimental designs.

Cross-sectional social surveys

Cross-sectional social surveys are often overlooked as a source of longitudinal information. The majority of the data in a cross-sectional social survey will relate to only one point in time. Cross-sectional social surveys sometimes collect a small amount of information that has a temporal dimension. For example, a cross-sectional survey might collect information on a respondent's current occupation and also on their father's occupation when they themselves were aged 14. While the information is collected at only one point in time, the measures still contain a temporal dimension and can inform analyses of social change (i.e. intergenerational occupational mobility). Similarly a respondent in a cross-sectional survey might be asked about their current job and also about their first job. These data could effectively be used to analyse intragenerational occupational change. The point here is that while the survey is cross-sectional, the measures collected contain some temporal information.

Many cross-sectional surveys are carried out on multiple occasions. These surveys are not based on repeated contacts with the same individuals (or households), but they offer the possibility of comparing similar data for different points in time. Combining data from repeated cross-sectional surveys is a particularly effective way to study trends over time. There are numerous large-scale repeated cross-sectional surveys. A notable example is the Labour Force Survey, which has been carried out in the UK since 1979 (and for which a similar survey is undertaken in many other countries). Further examples are the General Household Survey, which commenced in the UK in 1971, and the Family Expenditure Survey, which dates back to the 1950s. The US Current Population Survey is another example of a repeated cross-sectional survey.

For many social science analyses, cross-sectional surveys provide highly appropriate temporal data on social patterns. Repeated cross-sectional surveys offer opportunities to analyse macro-level trends, sometimes extending over lengthy periods of time. They do not, however, offer any insights into micro (i.e. individual)-level changes over time. This is because cross-sectional surveys generally do not include information that links up individuals in the surveys at different time points. We will return to the analysis of multiple cross-sectional surveys for quantitative longitudinal social science data analysis in Chapter 3.

Longitudinal social surveys with repeated contacts

Central to the collection of longitudinal social survey data is the concept of a panel. A panel is a sample of respondents who are contacted and surveyed on multiple occasions. The idea of researching a panel of respondents was pioneered by sociologist Paul Lazarsfeld for opinion research in the 1930s (see Lazarsfeld and Fiske, 1938). The sample unit will usually consist of individuals, but could also consist of households, firms, farms, schools or hospitals, or any other unit of social science research interest.

A cohort study is a special type of panel study. It is principally concerned with charting the development, or progress, of a particular group from a certain point in time. A notable example is a birth cohort. This form of study tracks or charts the development of a group of babies born in a particular year and follows them through childhood and into adulthood.

In Britain we are richly furnished with birth cohort datasets and we will outline the main studies later.

Not all cohort datasets track individuals from birth. For example, the Youth Cohort Study of England and Wales (YCS) monitored the behaviour and decisions of representative samples of young people aged 16 and upwards as they made the transition from compulsory education to further or higher education, or into the labour market (Gayle, Murray and Connelly, 2016). The British Medical Association Cohort Study of Medical Graduates (2006) followed a group of new doctors, who were all at the same career stage, and tracked them from qualification through the first ten years of their professional careers.

The term 'balanced panel' is used to describe a dataset where every respondent has the same number of repeated contacts. Balanced panels are more common in experimental situations where the study is specifically designed to collect the same number of data points for each participant. 'Unbalanced panels' are ubiquitous in longitudinal social surveys. This is because routinely some individuals leave the study, new participants enter the study and some participants will not have provided data at every wave. Unbalanced panel data are far more usual in the social sciences, therefore in Chapter 5 we will concentrate on methods that can be applied to unbalanced repeated contacts data.

Modes of survey data collection

It is useful to distinguish between two forms of temporal data collection. Prospective data are collected as the study moves forward. Measures are collected at each subsequent contact, for example in annual interviews. By contrast, retrospective data contain historic or 'back-dated' information. For example, when a new study begins, participants might be asked to supply retrospective information on their employment history from the time that they entered the labour market up to their present job. Most of the large-scale longitudinal social surveys have prospective designs, but in practice also collect some retrospective data.

Historically, interviews and traditional questionnaires were common in large-scale longitudinal studies but multiple modes of data collection are now usual. Data collection has been enhanced by computer-aided interviewing techniques, and electronic communication strategies are increasingly being used to collect data in large-scale longitudinal studies.

The Research value of repeated contacts quantitative longitudinal data

At the beginning of his insightful chapter on longitudinal social science data analysis, Davies (1994) states that researchers are more likely to be encouraged to analyse longitudinal data if they understand its research value. In this section we will introduce the main research benefits of quantitative longitudinal data.

Micro-level dynamics

We will begin with a vignette.

Jason Jones is aged 10. One day he comes home from school and he notices that his Dad's car is not outside of his house. Jason goes into his house and finds his Mum standing in the kitchen crying. Jason's Mum informs him that his Dad has left them. Jason's Dad rapidly loses contact with the family and does not provide any financial support. They are plunged into poverty and family life becomes very difficult.

One day, a few years later, Jason returns from school and he notices that an unfamiliar car is parked outside of his house. He enters his house and his Mum introduces him to her new 'friend', a man called Mike. Mike is very friendly and starts spending time at Jason's house. After a while he buys Jason an Xbox. Later that year Jason and his Mum go on holiday with Mike. Shortly after, Mike comes to live with Jason and his Mum, and their financial position improves dramatically. Life for Jason and his Mum gets much better.

One day, about a year later, Jason returns from school and notices that Mike's car is not outside. He enters his house and finds his Mum is in the kitchen crying. Jason glances into the sitting room and notices that his Xbox is gone.

It is easy to guess what has happened, and we can speculate on the likely changes to Jason and his Mum's life and their financial situation.

This snapshot into the life of young Jason Jones is disheartening, but we have chosen it because it provides a vivid illustration of our first methodological point. Imagine that data were collected on the Jones family via a cross-sectional survey at any time during the period of this vignette. The cross-sectional survey would accurately collect information on the family's current circumstances, and a little retrospective information might also be collected. It is unlikely that with cross-sectional information a researcher could genuinely understand the journey that Jason and his mother have been on. Understanding the micro-level social processes that are associated with the flows into and out of childhood poverty is an example of a research area that cannot be properly studied without comprehensive temporal information.

Many other social phenomena are inherently temporal in their nature. For example, family migration is intrinsically linked to the movement from one place at a certain time to another place at a later point in time. Nowok et al. (2013) is one example of a study that uses repeated contacts data to study family migration. This study found that on average UK migration was preceded by a period when individuals experienced a measureable decline in happiness for a variety of reasons and migration itself caused a boost in happiness, and brought people back to their initial levels.

Another situation where temporal information is required is the study of individual development. Bergman and Magnusson (1990) describe longitudinal data as the lifeblood of the study of individual development (e.g. in childhood), and it has been pointed out many times that the most important questions concerning individual development can only be answered by adopting a longitudinal design whereby the same individuals are followed through time. Turner, Alborz and Gayle (2008) provide an example of the research value of repeated contacts data for studying individual development. Their study analysed data on children with Down's syndrome and their families. Their findings suggest that notwithstanding the dominant effect of the severity of intellectual impairment, a number of factors within and outside the family may also contribute to higher attainment in reading, writing and numeracy. In particular, mainstream schooling for those with less severe disabilities appears to have benefitted the children in this study.

Temporal ordering of events

The 'arrow of time' flies in only one direction. Experiences at nursery school could affect a young person's chances of going to university. Teenage smoking could influence health in old age. We cannot conceive of circumstances where university entry could influence experiences at nursery school or how health in old age could influence smoking behaviour decades before. The reversal of the arrow of time would render the external social world nonsensical. Repeated contacts longitudinal data help facilitate the accurate temporal ordering of information, which can inform narratives about the direction of influence. Research studies have routinely taken advantage of the 'arrow of time' and have used longitudinal data to investigate the direction of social influences.

The association between ill health and unemployment serves as a useful example (see Bartley, 1994). This association is consistent with both the theoretical claim that unemployment causes ill health and the alternative theoretical claim that ill health causes unemployment.

Table 1 shows a hypothetical panel of data on ill health and unemployment. Repeated contacts data were collected each month (for 12 months) from Person A. This respondent had relatively good health at the start of the study. Their level of health was 17 on a scale where 20 is very good health. Person A was employed for the first three months of the study and

Table 1 Hypothetical data on ill health and unemployment (Person A)

Month	Level of health (20 = very good health)	Employment status
1	17	Employed
2	17	Employed
3	17	Employed
4	17	Unemployed
5	17	Unemployed
6	10	Unemployed
7	9	Unemployed
8	5	Unemployed
9	4	Unemployed
10	3	Unemployed
11	2	Unemployed
12	1	Unemployed

became unemployed in month 4. We observe that their health started to decline in month 6 and deteriorated to level 1 by the end of the study. This pattern is consistent with the theoretical claim that becoming unemployed negatively affected their health.

Table 2 shows another hypothetical series of data on ill health and unemployment. Repeated contacts data were collected each month (for 12 months) from Person B. This respondent also had relatively good health at the start of the study. Their level of health was 17 on a scale where 20 is very good health. Person B was employed for the first three months of the study and became unemployed in month 4. We observe that their health started to decline in month 2 and deteriorated to level 1 by the end of the study. This pattern is consistent with the theoretical claim that their ill health affected their employment status.

Despite the very different temporal ordering of events, if both of these people were included in a cross-sectional survey in month 12, Person A would have been unemployed for 9 months and have a health score of 1 and Person B would also have been unemployed for 9 months and have a health score of 1. This is an obvious example of how panel (i.e. repeated contacts) data can make an essential contribution to untangling micro-social processes.

Table 2 Hypothetical data on ill health and unemployment (Person B)

Month	Level of health (20 = Very good health)	Employment status
1	17	Employed
2	1	Employed
3	1	Employed
4	1	Unemployed
5	1	Unemployed
6	1	Unemployed
7	1	Unemployed
8	1	Unemployed
9	1	Unemployed
10	1	Unemployed
11	1	Unemployed
12	1	Unemployed

Residual heterogeneity

There is another important benefit of repeated contacts data, which is more subtle and less immediately obvious. Data collection instruments often fail to capture the detailed nature of social life, and there is, almost inevitably, considerable variation (or heterogeneity) in response variables even among respondents that share the same characteristics across all of the explanatory variables that are included in an analysis. This is sometimes referred to as 'residual heterogeneity'. An alternative term is 'omitted variable bias', because hypothetically the heterogeneity could be captured by other important measures that should have been included in the model. A technical account of this issue is provided by Hedeker and Gibbons (2006).

Within social science studies some variables will inevitably be unmeasured so they cannot be included in an analysis. Some variables may even be unmeasurable in the context of a survey and cannot ever be collected (and therefore cannot be included in an analysis). As long as we make the assumption that (at least some of) these residual effects are enduring, there are techniques for providing increased control for the effects of omitted explanatory variables if we have repeated contacts data. We will elaborate on these techniques later.

State dependence

Economist J. J. Heckman stated in his Nobel lecture that a frequently noted empirical regularity in the analysis of unemployment data is that those who were unemployed in the past are more likely to be unemployed in the future and those who worked in the past are more likely to be working in the future (Heckman, 2001). Much of human behaviour is influenced by previous behaviour and outcomes (i.e. there is positive 'feedback'). This is known as 'state dependence'.

State dependencies are relatively easy to conceptualize. For example, if you are employed in May you are more likely to be employed in June. Similarly if you are currently married you are very likely to be married next year, and if you travel to work by car this week you are more likely to travel to work by car next week. McGinnis (1968) outlined the 'axiom of cumulative inertia'. The axiom states that the probability of remaining in any state increases as a strict monotonic function of the duration of prior residence in that state. Panel data open up the possibility of explicitly including past behaviour (and duration in a state) within a statistical modelling framework in order to better understand substantive outcomes.

Age, period and cohort effects

It is a stylized fact that older people are more conservative in their political attitudes (see Glenn, 1974). Do people simply become more conservative as they age? In the contemporary era, is it just that a conservative attitude fits more naturally with the interests of older people? Or have older cohorts been raised in less liberal times and maintained their more conservative political attitudes? A further benefit of longitudinal data is that they facilitate the exploration of the effects of three distinct but related temporal processes; these are ageing, time period and cohort membership. In this context the term 'cohort' describes a common group that is being studied. The term 'age' describes the amount of time since the cohort was constituted. The term 'period' describes the moment of observation. As Yang and Land (2008) assert, a common goal of age-period-cohort analyses is to assess the effects of one of the three factors on some outcome of interest, net of the influences of the other two time-related dimensions.

Age effects represent the variation associated with different age groups that is brought about by changes in circumstances (e.g. the accumulation of social experience, or human capital). This contrasts with period effects, which affect all age groups simultaneously (e.g. a societal change or a change in a policy). Cohort effects are associated with changes across groups of individuals who experience an initial event at the same time (e.g. they are all born in the same year or qualify as doctors at the same time). Cohort effects may be present because individuals had the same formative experiences (e.g. they grew up in Britain immediately after the Second World War, or they attended medical school at about the same time and received similar training).

The tangled effects of ageing, period and cohort membership can be present in both longitudinal and cross-sectional datasets. In general it is possible to make some inroads into distinguishing between these effects with data that have information on people from the same cohort at different ages. Statistical models that attempt to separate the independent effects of age, period and cohort encounter inherent identification problems; this is because *age = period − cohort*, and therefore, knowing the value of any two of these time-related factors can automatically determine the value of the third. This creates a serious problem in the attempt to decompose the effects of the three time-related influences in a single analytical framework (e.g. a standard statistical model) (see Harper, 2015; Glenn, 1976). More recently a number of advanced techniques have been proposed to help to deal with the problem of identification in age-period-cohort models. Yang and Land (2008) assert that advanced methodological guidance is needed to address the fundamental question of how to determine whether the phenomenon of interest is cohort based or whether some other factors, such as age or calendar year, are more relevant.

Conclusions

The research value of quantitative longitudinal data lies in the variety of important analytical contributions that they can make to addressing social research questions. Temporal data are clearly required to support statements about social trends and macro-level change. The capacity of repeated contacts data to better elaborate micro-level social processes is an obvious attraction. The ability to place events in a correct sequence and therefore to enable a better understanding of their temporal ordering is another key attraction of panel data analysis. The capacity to support analyses that have improved control for residual heterogeneity and state dependence is also a desirable feature of panel data. In principle it is possible to make some inroads into distinguishing between age, period and cohort effects with longitudinal data, but in our experience this is not always straightforward in practice.

2 Quantitative longitudinal datasets

In this chapter we will outline a range of quantitative longitudinal data resources that are suitable for social science research. The UK is home to the world's largest household panel study and longest-running large-scale birth cohort study. The Cohort and Longitudinal Studies Enhancement Resources (CLOSER) project aims to maximize the use of UK longitudinal data resources. Information on the UK's quantitative longitudinal data resources is regularly updated on the CLOSER website.[1] Rafferty et al. (2015) provide a useful introduction to UK data resources suitable for longitudinal data analyses.

Large-scale panel studies

The longest-running large-scale quantitative longitudinal dataset with a household panel design is the US Panel Study of Income Dynamics (PSID). PSID began in 1968 and is sometimes seen as the grandparent of all of the household panel surveys (Hill, 1992). The German Socio-Economic Panel (GSOEP) began in the mid-1980s (Burkhauser and Wagner, 1993). It follows a similar design to the PSID but benefitted from many of the methodological lessons that had been learnt. The GSOEP can be thought of as the elder sibling of the British Household Panel Survey (BHPS). Several nations now collect household panel data; these include the Household, Income and Labour Dynamics in Australia (HILDA) survey, the Swiss Household Panel (SHP) and the Canadian Survey of Labour and Income Dynamics (SLID) (see Wooden, Freidin and Watson, 2002; Budowski et al., 2001; Webber, 1994).

---

1 See http://www.closer.ac.uk/ (accessed 6 April 2016).

The British Household Panel Survey

The BHPS was a major panel study which began in 1991 (Taylor et al., 1996). It is available from the UK Data Archive (Study Number 5151). Members of the BHPS have now been incorporated into a larger study called Understanding Society (the UK Household Longitudinal Study), which will be discussed below. The BHPS was a multipurpose, or omnibus, survey that provided data resources suitable for investigating a wide range of research questions from across the social sciences. It followed a representative sample of individuals (the panel) for nearly two decades. The BHPS was based on yearly contacts with the households, usually in the autumn. It used an interview methodology where all members of sampled households aged 16 and above were interviewed for approximately 45 minutes each. There was an additional short household questionnaire which only one member of the household completed.

The BHPS sample was originally a stratified design drawn from records of postal addresses. All residents present at the selected addresses at the first wave of the survey were designated as panel members. These same individuals were re-interviewed each successive year. If they split away from the original household to form new households, they were still followed. All adult members of their new households were also interviewed. This was a very important feature of the BHPS design because it led to more wide-ranging data collection. In addition, the original survey was supplemented with new booster samples (which will be discussed below). The original BHPS survey contained 10,264 respondents (4,833 men and 5,431 women) in Wave A (1991) who were living in 5,511 households. By 2008 (Wave R) there were 14,419 respondents living in 8,144 households. By the time of the formal end of the BHPS, 43,272 adults had been interviewed at some time during the 18 waves of the survey.

The BHPS questionnaire covered a broad range of social science and policy interests. The topics included housing composition, housing conditions, residential mobility, education and training, health and the use of health services, labour market behaviour, socio-economic values, and income from employment, benefits and pensions. A core of questions were asked annually but some questions were asked less frequently. New questions were sometimes introduced and they often followed on from changing policies and changing research agendas. The variable component of the BHPS has included questions on wealth and assets, additional health measures, ageing in retirement, quality of life, children and parenting, views on crime and neighbourhood, and social networks. Buck et al. (1994) showcase the wide range of topics that can be analysed using the BHPS data.

The BHPS was a prospective design with yearly contacts (i.e. an interview usually conducted each autumn). Time-constant information such as the person's ethnicity or their place of birth, which are not expected to change, were asked only at the first point of contact when a respondent entered the panel. The BHPS also contained retrospective data collection exercises. For example, respondents were asked about their marital histories, their fertility histories and their work-life histories. New entrants to the survey (e.g. someone entering a BHPS household in the third wave) may be asked retrospective questions out of the usual sequence, but considerable background work went into the harmonization of life history data that predates the survey.

A specific youth questionnaire was introduced into the BHPS in 1994, and this is known as the British Youth Panel. Young people entered this sample at age 11 and exited at age 15, when they entered the adult survey. The design is known as a 'rotating' panel design because the new 11-year-olds grew into the panel and 15-year-olds grew out of it. A more detailed account of the youth data is provided by Gayle (2005).

Towards the end of the 1990s following territorial devolution in the UK, extension samples were introduced into the BHPS. These are commonly known as 'booster samples'. Living in Britain was the original survey name of the BHPS and the booster samples are sometimes referred to as Living in Scotland, Living in Wales and Living in Northern Ireland. The extension samples allowed for territory (i.e. country)-specific research and comparative research within the UK to be undertaken. For example, using the Scottish booster sample it became possible to undertake both Scotland-specific analyses and research comparing Scotland with England. Laurie and Wright (2000) provide detailed information on the Scottish booster sample. In Wave I (1999) 1,458 new Scottish and 1,428 new Welsh households were added to the BHPS. In Wave K (2001) another booster sample in Northern Ireland was collected. Ermisch and Wright (2005) have compiled a special volume of research papers using the Scottish booster sample data.

UK Household Longitudinal Study – Understanding society

The BHPS was greatly extended and subsumed into the UK Household Longitudinal Study (UKHLS), which is also known as *Understanding Society* (Buck and McFall, 2012). The UKHLS shares common design features and data collection characteristics with the BHPS. It began in January 2009 and contains approximately 40,000 UK households, and is currently the largest household panel survey in the world. Hobcraft and Sacker (2011) provide an overview of the origins and development of the UKHLS. The UKHLS is available from the UK Data Archive (Study Number 6614).

The UKHLS is organized into a core of annual questions and topical modules which are rotated. The annual core makes up about half of the interview and collects information on important events that occurred between interviews. Many UKHLS questions were also asked in the BHPS and they facilitate continued longitudinal analyses of the BHPS data. An outline of the questionnaire content of the annual repeated measures, the rotating modules, the ethnic minority boost and the youth self-completion questionnaire is provided in Buck and McFall (2012 see Tables 1 and 2).

Buck and McFall (2012) highlight five key areas in which the UKHLS extends the research scope of the BHPS. First, the survey's very large sample size permits the study of research questions for which other longitudinal datasets are too small to effectively support analyses. For example, it better enables analyses at subregional levels and supports analyses of the geographical variations in policies (e.g. in the different territories of the UK). The large sample size also facilitates analyses of groups that usually have low coverage in nationally representative surveys, for example people living with disabilities or young mothers.

Second, the UKHLS contains an ethnic minority booster sample (which oversamples respondents from ethnic minorities) and collects additional measurements relevant to their social and economic experiences of living in Britain (see Berthoud et al., 2009). Third, data are collected on a wide range of research topics. While the main focus of the study is social and economic life, a much broader array of data are collected on health, well-being, psychological attributes, social attitudes and environmental behaviour.

Fourth, the UKHLS collects an innovative range of health indicators and biomeasures. For an introduction to the role and collection of these measures in social surveys, see Weinstein, Vaupel and Wachter (2007) and Jaszczak, Lundeen and Smith (2009). Fifth, the UKHLS includes a special panel of approximately 1,500 households, which is known as the Innovation Panel (UK Data Archive Study Number 6949). The Innovation Panel is extremely valuable because it allows methodological developments to be tested within a realistic survey context, which mirrors the main UKHLS survey. The Innovation Panel informs decisions for the main survey but it also provides a platform for methodological research. Details on some of the early experimental and non-experimental studies conducted as part of the Innovation Panel are reported by Uhrig (2011).

The UKHLS comprises four main components. These are the general population survey, the ethnic minorities booster sample, the BHPS and the Innovation Panel. The ethnic minority booster sample was designed to provide samples of about 1,000 adults in five large minority ethnic groups in the UK (Indian, Pakistani, Bangladeshi, Caribbean and African) (Berthoud et al., 2009). Estimates from social surveys were used to identify geographical areas with an ethnic minority density of at least 5 per cent. Samples were drawn from these high-density sectors and households were initially screened for the presence of a member of a minority ethnic group.

Respondents from the BHPS entered the UKHLS in the second wave. The inclusion of the BHPS sample is scientifically important because it preserves the ongoing and already established panel of household data. The inclusion of the BHPS has lengthened the temporal coverage of the UKHLS data. As far as possible the Innovation Panel mirrors the main UKHLS sample. The Innovation Panel does not include households in Northern Ireland or households in the north of Scotland.

The overall target for the achieved initial sample was 40,000 households: approximately 26,000 from the general population sample, approximately 4,000 from the ethnic minority boost, approximately 8,400 from the BHPS and approximately 1,500 from the Innovation Panel. At the start of the study the total achieved number of households across the four samples was 39,802 containing 101,086 adults and children (Buck and McFall, 2012, 11). Further details are provided in Burton, Laurie and Lynn (2011).

The four main sample designs are similar and are multistage designs.[2] Lynn (2009b) details the unique features of each of the UKHLS samples,

---

2 For an introduction to these methods of sampling and selection see (De Vaus, 2013) and for a more extended and technical review see Moser and Kalton (1971).

which we summarize below. The general population survey is a stratified, clustered equal probability sample of residential addresses drawn to a uniform design throughout all of the UK (including the north of Scotland). The Northern Irish sample is not clustered, however. Within Great Britain the primary sampling units are postal sectors. They are stratified by the nine official regions of England, plus Scotland and Wales, by population density and by ethnic minority density. This resulted in the systematic selection of 2,640 postal sectors with probability proportional to size (number of addresses). Within each sampled sector, 18 addresses were selected systematically, resulting in an equal probability sample of 47,520 addresses in Great Britain. In Northern Ireland 2,400 addresses were selected systematically from the Land and Property Services Agency list of domestic properties.

The overall response rate at the first wave for the general population survey was 57.2 per cent and for the ethnic minority boost was 56.9 per cent. The response rate for the general population was slightly lower than the 60 per cent target, but the ethnic minority boost was slightly higher than the 55 per cent target. These rates are common for omnibus surveys in the UK (Buck and McFall, 2012). Burton Laurie and Lynn (2011) provide in-depth information on the UKHLS response rates.

The constraints of undertaking such a large data collection exercise meant that the UKHLS fieldwork is spread over a 2-year period. The overall sample was partitioned into 24 monthly subsamples, each independently representative of the UK population. This means that differences over time within a wave can be compared using nationally representative subsamples, and it also means that quarterly or annual subsets of the data can be analysed independently.

There are three categories of respondents in the UKHLS. First, there are respondents who were in households at the start of the study, they are designated as original sample members (OSM). Every OSM will be followed throughout the life of the UKHLS as long as they continue to live in the UK. A child born to an OSM is automatically an OSM and is followed in the usual way. Second, there are individuals who join a household that includes an OSM. They are also interviewed in the study and they are designated as temporary sample members (TSM). For example, when an adult male OSM moves in with his female partner she will also be interviewed and will become a TSM. A TSM is not followed when they no longer live in a household with an OSM. The third type of respondent is a permanent sample member (PSM). If a male TSM fathers a child with an OSM he becomes a PSM and remains potentially eligible for interview for the life of survey (Knies, 2014). This categorization of members and the 'following rules' are designed to mimic the demographic processes by which the population is reproduced. This includes births, deaths, partnership formations and dissolutions, and emigration. Therefore, the study's 'following rules' provide an organic selection method which over time represent the evolving pattern of families and households in the UK.

Computer-aided personal interviewing is the main method of data collection, although several data collection instruments are used. One household member completes the household enumeration grid, which collects general information and then provides the household interview, which takes about 15 minutes to complete. The adult household members (those aged 16+) undertake a personal interview which is usually completed in 32 minutes. The adult household members also undertake a self-completion questionnaire which usually takes less than 10 minutes to complete. There is a short proxy interview about adults who are unavailable for the interview. Information on children under the age of 10 is provided by a responsible adult (e.g. a parent) as part of the adult and household interviews. Respondents aged 10–15 are asked to fill in a self-completion questionnaire, which is a paper-and-pencil instrument.

Some versions of the UKHLS are available via secure access, for example a version with linked data on detailed localities and other selected characteristics (UK Data Archive Study Number 6676) (see Rabe, 2011). These new resources are beneficial and, for example, Clark et al. (2014) use the spatial data linked to the survey data to explore life events and travel behaviour.

The depth and breadth of research questions that can be investigated with the UKHLS data are easy to illustrate. For example, Green, Poland and Willis (2016) studied companionship and community networks of older LGBT adults. Davillas, Benzeval and Kumari (2016) used the UKHLS to examine the association between body mass index and mental health. Clark and Coulter (2015) examined personal attitudes and attachments to neighbourhood. Chan and Ermisch (2015) used the data to study how close 'middle-aged' couples live to their parents. Zwysen (2015) studied the effects of a father's worklessness on young adults in the UK. McAloney et al. (2014) used the data to examine the smoking habits of young people and their mothers.

Cohort studies

Cohort studies are common in the social sciences and in health and medical research. A cohort study is a special case of a panel study. The panel is made up of a group of individuals who share a common characteristic or experience. The birth cohort study is a specific type of panel study where a group of individuals born around the same time are studied. Birth cohort studies can be found as geographically far afield as the Aberdeen Children of the 1950s Cohort Study (see Batty et al., 2004), the Stockholm Birth Cohort Study (see Stenberg and Vågerö, 2006), the US Early Childhood Longitudinal Study (see Flanagan and West, 2004), Growing Up in Australia: The Longitudinal Study of Australian Children (see Gray and Sanson, 2005) and Growing Up in New Zealand (see Morton et al., 2013).

The major British cohort studies

Britain is unique insofar as it has an unparalleled collection of large-scale nationally representative long-running birth cohort studies. A useful resource for getting preliminary information on British cohort datasets is the Cohort Directory,[3] which is a searchable tool for some of the main UK cohort studies. A useful review is also provided by the Medical Research Council (see MRC, 2014).

The first of the British birth cohort studies was the 1946 National Birth Cohort, MRC National Survey of Health and Development (NSHD). It is currently the longest-running birth cohort study in the world (Pearson, 2016). The study aimed to address social and health policy questions in the years directly preceding the establishment of the UK National Health Service in 1948. The initial survey was a systematic sample of babies born in a single week in March 1946.

Data collection was frequent during infancy and the school years because of the pace of development and growth. Initial data were collected at birth and then the participants were re-contacted at ages 2 and 4. These two early childhood sweeps of data collection were primarily concerned with socio-economic differences in the infant's growth, development, and morbidity, and with the effect of care and the family's socio-economic

---

3 See https://www.mrc.ac.uk/research/facilities/cohort-directory/ (accessed 6 April 2016).

circumstances upon health outcomes. During the school years the measurement of growth and health continued alongside a new stream of data collection focusing on education. In the youth phase measures relating to educational outcomes were collected, alongside data on topics such as delinquency. In the early adult phase collecting data on education, occupations and income came to the fore. In the middle phases of adulthood the study's health data collections were re-oriented. The focus became the measurement of physical and mental function, morbidity and mortality.

Wadsworth et al. (2006) provide a profile of the 1946 cohort, and Pearson (2016) has recently produced a popular science book on the cohort. The NSHD is accessible from the MRC Unit for Lifelong Health and Ageing. The data in the 1946 cohort has led to several landmark studies. Douglas and Blomfield (1958) showcased the first waves of data from the NSHD and charted the pre-school lives of the cohort. The study revealed that social and economic circumstances were generally improving in Britain but there was still a high degree of social inequality that affected the health of children in disadvantaged families. Douglas (1964) focused on primary school experiences and the transition to secondary school. This study was important because it provided empirical evidence that parents and pre-school circumstances had a substantial impact on outcomes in primary school, and this revealed high levels of social inequality. Douglas, Ross and Simpson (1968) focused on experiences and outcomes in secondary education and revealed enduring social inequality in the British education system. More recently, and reflecting the collection of data across the life course, studies such as Kuh et al. (2013) have used the data to study healthy ageing.

The second of the major British birth cohort studies was the 1958 National Child Development Study (NCDS). It mirrored the design of the 1946 study. The initial aims of the study were to address concerns regarding stillbirths and neonatal deaths. The cohort is a systematic sample of babies born in one week of March 1958. The original survey was not planned as a longitudinal study but funding became available to retrace the cohort. Further data collection exercises took place when the cohort members were 7, 11, 16, 23, 33, 42, 46, 50 and 55 and data continue to be collected.

The omnibus nature of the data collected on the 1958 cohort means that it has become an invaluable data source on such diverse topics as the effects of socio-economic circumstances on health, social mobility and changes in social attitudes. The NCDS is an exceptional resource for studying ageing and changes over the lifecourse. Power and Elliott (2006) provide a profile of the 1958 cohort. Butler and Bonham (1963) provide a useful account of the origins of the study, and Davie, Butler and Goldstein (1972) provide useful results from the early phase of the study. The data can be accessed from the UK Data Archive (Study Number GN 33004).

The NCDS data have been used in a wide variety of applications across social science disciplines and in health research. For example, Furstenberg and Kiernan (2001) used the data to compare children who experienced parental divorce in childhood with those who were young adults when their parents divorced, to examine long-term effects of divorce. Bartley, Kelly and Sacker (2012) examined the relationship between financial adversity in childhood and lung function in midlife, and Gregg and Tominey (2005) examined the effects of youth unemployment on earnings in later life.

The genealogy of publications also reflect the lifecourse of the cohort. Bynner (1999) studied youth transitions, Berrington and Diamond (2000b) studied marriage and cohabitation patterns, Elliott (2002) studied women's employment behaviour after childbirth and Deary et al. (2013) investigated cognitive ability in middle age. The flexibility of the NCDS is illustrated by studies such as Elliott (2013), who undertook qualitative biographical interviews with a subsample of 170 members of the cohort.

The third of the major British birth cohort studies was the 1970 British Cohort Study (BCS70). Following the initial birth survey the cohort were followed up at ages 5, 10, 16, 26, 30, 38 and 42. The BCS70 mirrored the design of the two earlier birth cohorts, and the initial sample consists of babies born in a single week of 1970. The BCS70 is an omnibus study and collects information on a broad spectrum of topics relating to social and economic life and health. Elliott and Shepherd (2006) provide a profile of the 1970 cohort, and Butler, Despotidou and Shepherd (1997) provide information on the early phase of the study. The data can be accessed from the UK Data Archive (Study Number GN 33229).

The BCS70 data have been used in a wide variety of applications across social science disciplines and in health research. For example, Stewart-Brown and Haslum (1988) studied partial sight in childhood. Bynner and Parsons (2002) examined school-to-work transitions. Cooksey et al. (2009) used the BCS70 data to examine the relationship between mothers' employment and child development in a comparative framework with US data. Cable, Sacker and Bartley (2008) investigated the effects of employment on psychological health in mid-adulthood. Viner and Taylor (2007) examined the adult outcomes of binge drinking in adolescence. There was then a gap in the collection of large-scale nationally representative birth cohort studies in Britain. The next major birth cohort study was the Millennium Cohort Study (MCS), which was set up to follow the lives of children born at the turn of the new century. Data have been collected at birth, 9 months and at ages 3, 5, 7 and 11 years. Fieldwork has now been completed for the age 14 survey and there are plans to carry out another survey at age 17. The MCS covers the usual topics that would be expected in a birth cohort study but also collects information on topics such as parenting, family income and social capital.

The design of the MCS differs from that of the earlier birth cohorts. It is a sample of babies born throughout the year. The MCS covers the whole of the UK rather than just the three territories of Great Britain, and has boosted samples in Scotland, Wales and Northern Ireland to allow adequate sample sizes for analyses within each territory. The sample is geographically clustered, with an over-representation of deprived areas, and this increases the scope for including community-level analyses (Smith and Joshi, 2002). A major difference between the MCS and the earlier birth cohorts is that it has a complex sample design and selection procedure (see Plewis et al., 2007, Ketende and Jones, 2011b). Connelly and Platt (2014) provide a profile of the MCS, and Hansen (2014) provides detailed information on the first five surveys. The data can be accessed from the UK Data Archive (Study Number GN 33359).

Dex and Joshi (2006) edited an extensive volume containing work on pregnancy, childbirth, social origins, childhood development, childcare, and employment and parenting. This was followed by Hansen, Joshi and Dex (2010), which is a more extensive volume of work covering the first five years of the lives of the MCS members. Platt et al. (2014) showcase findings from the age 11 survey.

The multidisciplinary nature of the MCS data supports a wide range of analyses. For example, Quigley, Kelly and Sacker (2007) investigated breastfeeding and hospitalization for diarrheal and respiratory infections. Kelly et al. (2009) examined variations in birth weight among ethnic groups. Sabates and Dex (2015) examined the impact of multiple risk factors on young children's cognitive and behavioural development. Connelly (2011a) examined the drivers of unhealthy weight in childhood, and Chanfreau et al. (2015) investigated the disparities in the take-up of school sports activities.

The similar structure and scope of the British Birth Cohorts has facilitated cross-cohort comparisons. Brown and Elliott (2010) offer an outline of the 1958 and 1970 cohorts, and demonstrate the potential for longitudinal analyses and cross-cohort comparisons. Bynner and Joshi (2002) studied inequality and opportunity in education using the NCDS and the BCS70 data. Breen and Goldthorpe (2001) studied social class, mobility and merit through a cross-cohort comparison of 1958 and 1970 data. Connelly (2011b) studied the influence of childhood test scores, and family background and occupational positions in adulthood using the NCDS and the BCS70.

Data from the 1946, 1958 and 1970 cohorts have been used by Bukodi and Goldthorpe (2011) to study returns to higher education and by Bukodi et al. (2015) to study social mobility. Chan and Boliver (2013) examined grandparental effects on social mobility using these datasets. Fertig (2010) used data from the NCDS, BCS and MCS to examine smoking behaviour, and Connelly and Gayle (2015) used these three cohorts to investigate changing socio-economic inequalities in childhood cognitive test performances.

Other British birth cohort studies

In addition to the major birth cohort studies, the UK data portfolio also includes some other large-scale birth cohorts. Growing Up in Scotland (GUS) is a birth cohort study following the lives of a large sample of children born in Scotland. It began in 2005 and collects a wide spectrum of information, for example on family circumstances, child development, health, pre-school experiences, education, physical activity and parenting styles. A description of the study is provided by Anderson et al. (2007). The data can be accessed from the UK Data Archive (Study Number SN 5760).

The GUS data have been used in a variety of social science and health projects. For example, Parkes, Sweeting and Wight (2015) used the GUS data to investigate parenting stress and parent support among mothers with high and low education. Parkes, Sweeting and Wight (2016) used the data to examine early childhood precursors and school age correlates on internalizing problem trajectories in young children. Parkes, Sweeting and Wight (2014) examined family and school influences on children's social and emotional well-being. Skafida and Treanor (2014) examined how family income predicts change in children's diets.

The Avon Longitudinal Study of Parents and Children (ALSPAC) is a birth cohort study with a regional focus. It considers multiple genetic, epigenetic, biological, psychological, social and other environmental exposures in relation to a similarly diverse range of health, social and developmental outcomes. The samples were recruited from the Avon area, which is in the Southwest of the UK. ALSPAC has a data-sharing and access policy and proposals to access data must be made through the ALSPAC Executive Committee.[4] A profile of the cohort is provided by Boyd et al. (2012).

ALSPAC has generally supported medical and health research but has also been used effectively in social science research. For example, Melotti et al. (2011) studied adolescent tobacco and alcohol use. Jerrim et al. (2013) undertook an innovative study of the socio-economic gradient in children's reading skills by examining the role of genetics. Mokrysz et al. (2016) studied the effect of cannabis use on education and intelligence.

Other longitudinal studies

There are a number of other longitudinal studies within the UK social science research data portfolio. In this section we review a small number of these data resources to illustrate the diversity of the existing quantitative longitudinal datasets.

The Youth Cohort Study of England and Wales (YCS) was a major longitudinal study that began in the mid-1980s. It was a large-scale nationally representative survey funded by the government and was designed to monitor the behaviour of young people as they reached the minimum school-leaving age and either remained in education or entered the labour market. The YCS survey collected detailed information on the young person's qualifications and experiences of education, as well as information on employment and training. A limited amount of information was collected on the young person's personal characteristics, their family and circumstances at home. The YCS sample was nationally representative of Year 11 pupils in England and Wales. A large sample from an academic year group (a cohort) was contacted in the spring following school Year 11. The young people were usually aged 16–17 when they were first contacted. The main data collection instrument was a postal questionnaire. The cohort

---

4 See http://www.bristol.ac.uk/alspac/researchers/access/ (accessed 14 June 2016).

members were usually re-contacted and surveyed on at least two further occasions (e.g. at ages 17–18 and 18–19).

Currently, 13 cohorts of YCS data can be accessed from the UK Data Archive (Study Number GN 33233). A special combined cohort dataset, which includes data on Scottish pupils, is also available from the UK Data Archive (Study Number 5765). The YCS was primarily a monitoring tool and was not specifically designed for social science research. A number of challenges are associated with analysing YCS data, most notably inadequate documentation (see Croxford, 2006). Despite these challenges a range of analyses usually orientated towards education and employment have been undertaken using the YCS. Drew, Gray and Sime (1992) is an example of analyses of the older cohorts, and Gayle, Murray and Connelly (2016) is an example of analyses that span a number of YCS cohorts.

The English Longitudinal Study of Ageing (ELSA) is a longitudinal study of a representative cohort of men and women living in England who were initially aged 50 years and above. ELSA was designed as a sister study to the US Health and Retirement Study. ELSA is multidisciplinary in its orientation and involves the collection of economic, social, psychological, cognitive, health, biological and genetic data. The study began in 2002 and data are usually collected at two-year intervals. Data are collected using computer-assisted personal interviews and self-completion questionnaires, with additional nurse visits for the collection of health and physical measures. ELSA is harmonized with ageing studies in other countries to facilitate international comparisons, and administrative data have been linked to the sample. Steptoe et al. (2013) provide a profile of the ELSA cohort. The data can be accessed from the UK Data Archive (Study Number GN 33368).

The Northern Ireland Cohort Longitudinal Study of Ageing (NICOLA) has recently been established. NICOLA will closely follow the comprehensive approaches undertaken by ELSA and The Irish Longitudinal Study of Ageing (TILDA). Anderson, Boyle and Sharp (2008) proposed a Scottish longitudinal study of ageing, and preparatory and pilot work for the Healthy Ageing in Scotland study is currently in progress. Kaiser (2013) provides a useful overview of a series of international studies and compares their methodologies and key policy themes and also outlines some key findings.

The UK is also uniquely served by three quantitative longitudinal studies based on census and administrative data. The longest running of the three is the Office for National Statistics Longitudinal Study (ONS-LS), which covers England and Wales. The ONS-LS is a longitudinal sample of around

1 per cent of the total population of England and Wales. It is a systematic sample of people born on four birthdates spaced across the calendar year. The ONS-LS contains data from the decennial UK Censuses and other sources including routine event registrations (e.g. births, deaths, immigration and embarkation). It has linked records at each UK Census since 1971 (for the people born on one of four selected dates in the calendar year). Therefore, the ONS-LS is usually considered as being a systematic sample. These four dates were used to update the sample at the 1981, 1991, 2001 and 2011 Censuses, and new ONS-LS members enter the study through birth and immigration if they are born on one of the four selected birth dates.

The ONS-LS began in 1971 and the dataset were created and are maintained by the ONS. Researchers can access the ONS-LS data either in approved safe environments or by remote access. Goldring and Newman (2010) provide a useful outline of the ONS-LS and a commentary on its research value. The data have supported a wide spectrum of social science and health analyses. For example, Platt, Simpson and Akinwale (2005) used the data to examine social change in minority ethnic populations. Sturgis and Buscha (2015) examined changes to social mobility. Boyle, Norman and Popham (2009c) used the data to examine social mobility and health, and Bartley and Plewis (1997) used the data to look at socio-economic differences in health.

More recently two longitudinal studies based on census and administrative data have been developed, one covering Scotland and another covering Northern Ireland. These two studies are similar in design to the English and Welsh data. Each of the three studies has a slightly different set of data access arrangements but follows a similar procedure and usually requires users to be trained, data analysis work to be carried out in a safe environment and research outputs to be given official clearance. Boyle et al. (2009b) provide a profile of the Scottish Longitudinal Study (SLS), and Ralston, Gayle and Lambert (2016) provide an example of a recent analysis using the SLS. O'Reilly et al. (2012) provide a profile of the Northern Ireland Longitudinal Study (NILS), and O'Reilly et al. (2015) provide an example of analyses using the NILS data.

Cross-national and comparative longitudinal studies

The collection of nationally representative social survey data in many different countries has sometimes enabled researchers to undertake cross-national and comparative longitudinal analysis. Some social surveys are deliberately designed to facilitate cross-national research. Others originate as national surveys, and only at a later stage is an attempt made to bring their data into a cross-national framework (see Harkness, Van De Vijver and Mohler, 2003, Harkness et al., 2008). Not all cross-national surveys have a longitudinal element; however, reflecting the sustained and substantial work that is involved in developing cross-nationally comparative survey instruments, many of the designed cross-national social survey resources have been maintained over a long period of time. This makes them suitable for longitudinal analysis (i.e. they feature repeated cross-sectional, or repeated contacts, designs). In particular, there have been a great many endeavours in generating cross-nationally comparative repeated cross-sectional data that are suited to comparing trends over time across different countries. One notable example is the Luxembourg Income Study (see Smeeding, Jesuit and Alkemade, 2002). There are many other similar projects, some of which we will discuss further in Chapter 3.

Any cross-national survey design faces considerable challenges in establishing the comparability of measures across countries. Some survey measures (e.g. age and gender) may have a natural equivalence across societies, but many other measurements (e.g. income, welfare benefits and education) will not be equivalent, and in some cases there may not be any agreed-upon international standards for collecting or comparing these measures (Connelly, Gayle and Lambert, 2016a). Therefore, researchers using datasets from multiple countries are forced to put a great deal of work into assessing and ensuring the comparability and equivalence of survey measures (see Hoffmeyer-Zlotnik and Warner, 2014; Jowell et al., 2007). Johnson (1998) provides a useful overview of the methodological issues associated with undertaking research with cross-national datasets. Burkhauser and Lillard (2005) provide a valuable account of the scope and limitations of a number of projects that have endeavoured to bring together cross-national social survey datasets.

While most research using panel surveys focus on one particular country, the existence of similar panel studies in several nations presents opportunities for internationally comparative research. Research designs sometimes involve bespoke comparisons between a small number of panel studies from different countries, based upon access to and analysis of the original data (e.g. Hadjar and Samuel, 2015). There have also been some explicit attempts to construct cross-national and comparative longitudinal panel survey datasets. Two notable examples are the European Community Household Panel (ECHP) and the European Union Survey of Income and Living Conditions (EU-SILC). The ECHP has now been discontinued (Frick et al., 2007). Lillard and Burkhauser (2006) provide an account of the Survey of Health, Ageing and Retirement in Europe, which is a multidisciplinary and cross-national dataset.

The Cross-National Equivalent File (CNEF) project is an attempt to bring together data, *ex post*, from ongoing panel studies. The origins of the CNEF are described in Burkhauser et al. (2000). The CNEF 1970–2013 contains equivalently defined variables from the BHPS, the HILDA Survey, the Korea Labor and Income Panel Study (KLIPS), PSID, the Russia Longitudinal Monitoring Survey (RLMS-HSE) (new in 2016), the SHP, SLID and the GSOEP.[5] It is likely that other studies will be included at a later date.

Conclusions

The steadily expanding wealth and volume of large-scale longitudinal social survey datasets means that many social research questions can be addressed by using these resources. Sometimes more than one data resource might be used to answer the same research question. In such cases it is not always clear which data resource is optimal, but considerations of the size of the dataset, and the resolution of the variables available in the dataset, are important. In general when the main interest is describing longer term social trends, repeated cross-sectional surveys are often the most feasible source of longitudinal data. For some studies, data collected from repeated contacts from the same individuals will be required. Cohort designs tend to favour the study of growth or development in specific contexts. Due to their design, household panels tend to be particularly flexible for investigating micro-level change in short time periods in a wider range of contexts.

5 See https://cnef.ehe.osu.edu/ (accessed 4 April 2016).

3 Temporal analysis with cross-sectional data

Introduction

At the beginning of Chapter 1 we stated that temporal data can be collected in cross-sectional surveys and therefore it is mildly misleading to assume that longitudinal analyses can never be undertaken with cross-sectional survey data. We begin this chapter with a simple example. There is no doubt that Welsh is one of Europe's most robust minority languages and its cultural influence and traditions remain relevant today, and they are embraced by new generations learning and using the language (Welsh Language Unit, 2012). A comparison of the 1891 UK Census and the 1981 UK Census shows that the percentage of Welsh speakers in Wales had fallen from 54 per cent to 19 per cent. In this example, data collected at two distinctive time points allow us to understand change over time. Comparing the 1981 UK Census with the 1991 UK Census we find that the percentage of Welsh speakers remained at 19 per cent and then increased slightly to 21 per cent in the 2001 UK Census. This simple example should illustrate that using multiple sources of cross-sectional data we have been able to investigate social change. Examining patterns using data collected at different time points should not be overlooked because results can be useful in determining empirical regularities.

In applied research, relatively straightforward analytical techniques can even be used to explore temporal patterns within one-off cross-sectional social surveys. One notable example that has supported a large amount of analysis is the famous 1972 Oxford Mobility Study (OMS) (Goldthorpe and Mills, 2008). The original OMS was a cross-sectional data collection exercise that contributed to an influential analysis of social change in two ways. First, it summarized data on social mobility based upon comparing data about its respondents' current jobs with retrospective information about jobs from earlier time periods (e.g. the respondents' fathers' jobs or the respondents' first jobs). Second, it uncovered trends in social mobility rates, by comparing the social mobility experiences of respondents from different birth cohorts contained within the study.

More generally, using multiple datasets from repeated cross-sectional surveys is an effective way to study trends (or stability) over time. This is the main focus of this chapter.

When analysing repeated cross-sectional data, social scientists sometimes concentrate upon summarizing trends at the macro-level. This might involve deriving summary statistics for each different repeated cross-sectional dataset, and then presenting a summary of those statistics in relation to the time point of the survey. An important piece of advice is that when this approach is used a research study will always benefit from basing its findings on as many data points as possible. In the area of social mobility research, where analysts summarize trends in social reproduction based on summary statistics from different datasets, researchers have stressed that increasing the number of data points substantially reduces the risk of erroneous conclusions that might arise from measurement or sampling errors associated with any one specific dataset (see Ganzeboom, Luijkx and Treiman, 1989; Breen, 2004; Lambert, Prandy and Bottero, 2007; Bernardi and Ballarino, 2016).

Repeated cross-sectional data are also often analysed at the micro-level, using pooled datasets that combine records from different years. In most situations, methods that are common in the analysis of cross-sectional data are used. The most notable difference is that the time period associated with the data becomes a particularly important explanatory variable within the analysis (an example is provided below). Firebaugh (1997) provides a useful reference text on analysing repeated cross-sectional data in this context.

Comparing survey measures

The main challenge involved in making meaningful comparative statements with survey measures that are collected at different time periods, or in different countries, centres on the 'equivalence' of measures. Does completing a degree in engineering have the same social significance for a woman in 2016 as it would have had in 1967? Or can the ethnic group category in the UK 2001 Census 'Black Caribbean' reasonably be compared with the category 'Coloured' in the 1972 General Household Survey?

Johnson (1998) provides a comprehensive review of alternative concepts of equivalence. The term 'measurement equivalence' is used to describe data that have been purposively collected and organized to easily facilitate direct comparisons (Ehling, 2003). The term 'meaning equivalence' invokes the comparison of locations according to their relative, contextual meaning (see Van Deth, 2003). As an illustration, the relative social advantage associated with having an MBA may be substantially less in the UK than in Burkina Faso. Therefore, an analysis prioritizing 'meaning equivalence' would regard MBAs held in the two countries as marking different relative levels of educational attainment. It is important to understand that the source of equivalence problems for longitudinal data often lies not with a change in how something has been recorded over time, but with a change in the underlying distribution of a measure in the population. This means that the appearance of 'measurement equivalence' may not be enough to ensure 'meaning equivalence'.

Researchers using measures from repeated cross-sectional surveys should place effort into understanding the equivalence of their data. This will inevitably draw upon both their own and others' expert knowledge within the substantive field, and it is therefore impossible to provide detailed advice on the equivalence of measures in specific surveys. The terms 'standardizing' and 'harmonizing' are used to describe the activities associated with making measures comparable (see Ehling, 2003). Hoffmeyer-Zlotnik and Warner (2014) provide an extended account of harmonizing variables, and Connelly, Gayle and Lambert (2016a) provide practicable advice on how to organize and analyse key variables in social survey research.

An example of analysing pooled cross-sectional surveys

In this section we provide a simple example of using pooled cross-sectional surveys. The data are from the YCS, which we introduced in Chapter 2. In this example we pool data from the first sweeps of the 1990, 1993, 1995, 1997 and 1999 cohorts (using data from UK Data Archive Study Number SN 5765). The YCS is actually a repeated contacts cohort study, but in this example we are using only the first record from its respondents in each cohort, and we are analysing these data as repeated cross-sections. While this might seem to complicate the definition of datasets, it is in fact quite common for influential social research to be undertaken through methods of repeated cross-sectional analysis while using data that was itself drawn from a wider, repeated contacts longitudinal design (Breen and Goldthorpe, 2001).

Historically, school pupils in England and Wales have undertaken a diet of examinations called the General Certificate of Secondary Education (GCSE) at the end of compulsory education (see Playford and Gayle, 2016). In this analysis the outcome variable of interest is the pupils' GCSE points score in Year 11 (which was the end of compulsory schooling). We also have information on the pupils' gender and their parents' social class, which is measured by a three-category version of the official UK socio-economic classification NS-SEC (see Rose, Pevalin and O'Reilly, 2005).

An attractive feature of undertaking analyses on pooled cross-sectional datasets is that standard techniques (e.g. linear regression models and logistic regression models) can be used. It is common to include variables that identify the source of the data (i.e. the cross-sectional survey) or the time point within the analysis. An obvious extension to simpler approaches is to estimate statistical models that include interaction effects to assess changes in the impact of explanatory variables at different time points (e.g. in different surveys).

A linear regression model estimated on the pooled data from the five YCS cohorts is reported in Figure 1. The results in Figure 1 show that across the time period the overall profile of school GCSE attainment has increased considerably. This is evident from the positive main effect for the school cohorts. Pupils that were surveyed in 1999 on average achieved a GCSE points score that was 13.6 points higher than that of their counterparts in

```
      Source |       SS          df       MS          Number of obs   =    62,910
-------------+------------------------------------    F(5, 62904)     =    948.14
       Model | 1359059.45          5   271811.89      Prob > F        =    0.0000
    Residual | 18033188.1     62,904   286.677924     R-squared       =    0.0701
-------------+------------------------------------    Adj R-squared   =    0.0700
       Total | 19392247.6     62,909   308.258716     Root MSE        =    16.932

------------------------------------------------------------------------------
     t0score |      Coef.   Std. Err.      t    P>|t|     [95% Conf. Interval]
-------------+----------------------------------------------------------------
 cohort_1993 |   5.143661   .2080184    24.73   0.000     4.735944    5.551377
 cohort_1995 |   9.365432   .2157778    43.40   0.000     8.942508    9.788357
 cohort_1997 |   8.334607   .2166697    38.47   0.000     7.909934    8.75928
 cohort_1999 |   13.63625    .225169    60.56   0.000     13.19492    14.07758
        male |  -3.119253   .1354489   -23.03   0.000    -3.384733   -2.853773
       _cons |   31.93301   .1675295   190.61   0.000     31.60465    32.26136
------------------------------------------------------------------------------
```

Figure 1 Stata output: Regression model (OLS) General Certificate of Secondary Education (GCSE) points score School Year 11 Youth Cohort Study of England and Wales

```
      Source |       SS           df       MS       Number of obs   =      62,910
-------------+----------------------------------   F(9, 62900)     =      528.05
       Model |  1362275.97          9  151363.996   Prob > F        =      0.0000
    Residual |  18029971.6      62,900  286.645018   R-squared       =      0.0702
-------------+----------------------------------   Adj R-squared   =      0.0701
       Total |  19392247.6      62,909  308.258716   Root MSE        =      16.931


      t0score |      Coef.   Std. Err.      t    P>|t|     [95% Conf. Interval]
-------------+----------------------------------------------------------------
  cohort_1993 |   5.511817   .2834742    19.44   0.000     4.956207    6.067427
  cohort_1995 |   9.901535   .2939396    33.69   0.000     9.325413    10.47766
  cohort_1997 |    8.92802   .2970979    30.05   0.000     8.345708    9.510333
  cohort_1999 |   14.16292   .3062392    46.25   0.000     13.56269    14.76315
         male |  -2.249934   .3110738    -7.23   0.000    -2.859639   -1.640229
male*cohort_1993 |  -.7883375   .4172608    -1.89   0.059    -1.606169    .0294943
male*cohort_1995 |  -1.156655   .4328531    -2.67   0.008    -2.005048   -.3082621
male*cohort_1997 |  -1.269568   .4341967    -2.92   0.003    -2.120594   -.4185414
male*cohort_1999 |  -1.137471   .4518282    -2.52   0.012    -2.023055   -.2518865
        _cons |   31.52792    .212347   148.47   0.000     31.11172    31.94412
```

Figure 2 Stata output: Regression model (OLS) General Certificate of Secondary Education (GCSE) points score School Year 11 Youth Cohort Study of England and Wales (cohort and gender interactions)

the 1990 survey (the reference category). On average male pupils scored 3.1 points lower than female pupils. The model reported in Figure 2 includes an interaction effect to assess changes in the impact of gender at each of the five time points (i.e. the five cohorts of pupils surveyed in the YCS).

Cross-national comparative research using repeated cross-sectional surveys

Many social surveys are deliberately coordinated internationally to aid comparative research, other existing survey data can be brought together at a later stage for the purpose of making cross-national comparisons. Hoffmeyer-Zlotnik and Warner (2014 Chapter 4) provide a review of a number of important examples. Many of these surveys can also make a contribution to longitudinal research. Figure 3 lists a number of examples of large-scale survey projects that provide opportunities for longitudinal analysis through repeated cross-sectional surveys. These examples encompass considerable volumes of micro-social data. For example, IPUMS-I boasts on its website that it provides access to data from 1960 covering 614 million people in 277 censuses from 82 countries! The examples listed in Figure 3 are selective, and many other relevant studies exist. While some of the resources that are listed are intended to be general

(1) Studies with an orientation to socio-economic and socio-demographic data

IPUMS-I	https://international.ipums.org/international/
NAPP	https://www.nappdata.org/napp/
Luxembourg Income Study	http://www.lisdatacenter.org/
ISMF	http://www.harryganzeboom.nl/ismf/index.htm
CASMIN	http://www.nuff.ox.ac.uk/Users/yaish/npsm/

(2) Studies with an orientation to social and political attitudes

European Social Survey	http://www.europeansocialsurvey.org/
International Social Survey Programme	http://www.issp.org/
World Values Survey	http://www.worldvaluessurvey.org/
Eurobarometer	http://www.gesis.org/eurobarometer-data-service/home/

(3) Studies in educational research

TIMSS / PIRLS	http://timss.bc.edu/
PISA	http://www.pisa.oecd.org/

Figure 3 Selected examples of large-scale cross-nationally harmonized repeated cross-sectional survey projects

purpose or 'omnibus' resources suitable for a variety of uses, some of the examples are illustrative of data that emerge from more specialist studies. Such studies are typically academic projects that construct comparable data with a specific research aim.

The studies listed in Figure 3[1] are examples that have already been subject to some degree of harmonization. An important example is the annual Labour Force Surveys, which have been carried out in standardized ways across countries since the 1980s. They have coverage in around 200 countries and territories across the world and are coordinated by the International Labour Office.[2] The Luxembourg Income Study offers coordinated access to micro-data for the analysis of selected Labour Force Surveys from different countries after harmonization work has already

---

1 Websites (accessed 1 June 2016).

2 See http://www.ilo.org/dyn/lfsurvey/lfsurvey.home (accessed 1 June 2016).

been undertaken (see Smeeding, Jesuit and Alkemade, 2002). A standard approach is to derive aggregate summary statistics from different Labour Force Surveys and explore trends in those aggregate records.

There are some important attractions to using cross-national surveys for longitudinal research. There are many surveys available for studying trends over time. There are well-known challenges of comparability and standardization of measures when working with cross-national repeated cross-sectional survey datasets (see Johnson, 1998; Burkhauser and Lillard, 2005; Hoffmeyer-Zlotnik and Warner, 2014; Connelly, Gayle and Lambert, 2016b). Despite these challenges many projects have successfully analysed trends over time (see Mayer, 2005). It is reasonably easy for academic researchers to gain access to international survey data from national or international data archives[3] or from the online resources that projects often provide (see Hoffmeyer-Zlotnik and Warner, 2014). The majority of studies listed in Figure 3 offer access to their micro-data for secondary research free, or at nominal cost, for non-commercial and not-for-profit uses.

Conclusions

Considerable progress can be made by investigating longer term social trends using repeated (or pooled) cross-sectional surveys. A clear benefit of analysing pooled or repeated cross-sectional surveys is that well-understood standard techniques such as linear regression and logistic regression models can be used. The most serious challenge when dealing with repeated cross-sectional surveys is ensuring that measures are sufficiently equivalent over time in order to allow realistic comparisons to be made. Researchers should also consider how best to represent temporal dimensions in their analyses.

---

3 See UK Data Service https://www.ukdataservice.ac.uk (accessed 1 June 2016).

4 The analysis of duration data

Introduction

Duration analyses are generally employed to analyse how long something remains in a particular state, for example how long do graduates remain in their first job after leaving university. The central idea in duration analyses is that there is a fundamental change from one state to another at a specific point in time. The change in state is marked by an event. The term 'event' is not usually used to describe a gradual change and the event must consist of a relatively sharp disjunction between what precedes and what follows (Allison, 1984).

Techniques suitable for modelling duration data are routinely known as duration models, survival models, Cox regression, Cox models, failure-time analysis, hazard models and event history analysis. These terms are often used interchangeably. The different names partly reflect the development of methods for the analysis of duration data in different academic disciplines.

The foundational paper on duration models is Cox (1972). Models for duration data allow the data analyst to assess the relative influence of a number of explanatory factors upon how long it takes for an event to occur. The utility of duration models is evident when we consider that the models have been used to study the lifetimes of machine components in engineering, the duration of unemployment in economics, the time taken to complete cognitive tasks in psychology, the lengths of tracks on a photographic plate in particle physics and survival times of patients in clinical trials (see Cox and Oakes, 1984).

In the social sciences Heckman and Borjas (1980) used duration modelling approaches to study unemployment, Blossfeld and Hakim (1997) studied female part-time employment and Mulder and Smits (1999) investigated first-time home ownership. In the area of marriage and cohabitation, Lillard, Brien and Waite (1995) studied premarital cohabitation and subsequent marital dissolution, Kiernan and Mueller (1998) undertook an analysis of divorce using the BHPS and the NCDS and Boyle et al. (2008) examined union dissolution using the Austrian Family and Fertility Survey (FFS). Using the BHPS Chan and Halpin (2002) examined the influence of gender role attitudes and the domestic division of labour on divorce, and Pevalin and Ermisch (2004) investigated mental health, union dissolution and re-partnering.

Measuring durations

There are three requirements for correctly determining duration. First, a starting time must be unambiguously defined. Second, time must have a defined unit of measurement. Third, the event must be clearly defined (Cox and Oakes, 1984).

We begin with a simple example relating to breastfeeding. The majority of both academic and non-academic writing on breastfeeding is profoundly in favour of the practice (Schmied and Lupton, 2001). The definition of exclusive breastfeeding is that the infant receives only breastmilk, and no other liquids or solids (except medicines or vitamins and mineral supplements). Imagine that a set of data on exclusive breastfeeding were being analysed three years after the babies were born. It is fair to assume that all of the babies would have finished exclusively breastfeeding. Indeed results from the 2010 UK Infant Feeding Survey[1] reported that across the UK the level of exclusive breastfeeding had decreased to one per cent six months after birth.[2]

In this example birth provides an unambiguous starting point, and the duration of exclusive breastfeeding would probably be measured in days or weeks. One standard measure of the outcome or event in breastfeeding research is the first time that formula, other liquids or solids are given to a baby. The duration (the number of days or weeks that the baby was exclusively breast fed) is a continuous measure and it would be possible to estimate a standard linear regression model. One option might be to

1 See http://www.hscic.gov.uk/catalogue/PUB08694/ifs-uk-2010-chap2-inc-prev-dur.pdf (accessed 7 June 2016).
2 Readers who are fans of the hit UK television comedy 'Little Britain' might, however, remember the character Harvey Pincher, who was breast fed for much longer than most children.

model the log of the durations as a continuous outcome. Using the log of the outcome variable is sometimes advised when the outcome variable has a pronounced positive skew, which is common for measures of duration. This model is sometimes referred to as the accelerated life model (Goldstein, 1999).

In analyses where the social process is complete, by which we mean that all of the sample have achieved the outcome, the accelerated life model is appropriate. Mortality analyses of veterans who fought in the First World War is one such example. Similarly we envisage that at the end of this century researchers studying mortality will have access to 'birth to death records' for the UK 1946 birth cohort. In genuine empirical social science studies it is common to have individuals for whom the event does not take place within the window of observation, and to address this methodological issue, more complex techniques of analysis are required.

Figure 4 is a diagram based on data from a hypothetical study of unemployment. The study began at month 0 and concluded 18 months later. During the 18-month observation window Person A exited unemployment (by gaining a full-time job) 3 months into the study, Person B did the same 15 months into the study and Person C finished their unemployment spell 18 months into the study. The measure of the unemployment duration for these three participants in the study is unproblematic. Person D did not exit unemployment until after the study ended, and a researcher would not have access to the precise time at which this happened. Person E never exited unemployment. The obvious question is what should the value of their duration of unemployment be for Person

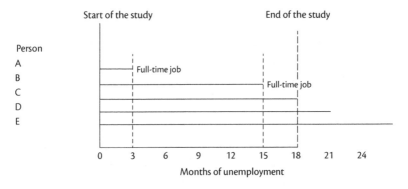

Figure 4 A diagram of a hypothetical study of unemployment

D and Person E? Both could be ascribed a duration value of 18 months. This would mean that Person C, who genuinely was unemployed for 18 months, would be treated similarly to Person D, who was unemployed for 21 months, and Person E, who in fact never exited unemployment. This method of approximation is evidently imperfect.

The durations for Person D and Person E are examples of censored data. Estimating a standard regression model using data which include censored observations is problematic because they do not have appropriate values for the duration measure. The impact on the results obtained using a standard regression model may sometimes be negligible. Plewis (1997) states that when there is a very small proportion of censored cases, they will have little effect and an accelerated life model might still be suitable. In our experience few supervisors, examiners and referees will be convinced that when there are censored observations this is a suitable approach!

The durations for Person D and Person E in Figure 4 are 'right censored'. Right-censored data are very typical in large-scale social science datasets. Data can also be left censored, which occurs when the observation window interrupts an ongoing process. Consider data from a study of romantic relationships. At the beginning of the study some couples may be just at the start of their relationship, but other couples will be in existing relationships that began long ago. Left-censored data are less common in social science datasets because it is often feasible to ask respondents retrospectively about the starting point of a relevant 'spell'. Studies such as the BHPS collect retrospective information, for example on marital relationships and job tenure.

Duration models

Cox (1972) proposed a modelling approach for analysing durations which include censored observations. The main technical feature of this modelling approach is that we no longer directly model the duration. In duration models the focus is on modelling the probability that an event occurs at time t, conditional on it not having occurred before t.

Here is a more intuitive explanation. Think of a professor walking down a corridor. We could ask the question: What is their probability of dying in the next nanosecond, given that they have not already died? A nanosecond later we could again ask the question: What is their probability of dying in the next nanosecond, given that they did not die in the previous nanosecond? Now imagine that we continued to make these probabilistic calculations repeatedly using these infinitesimal periods between two time points. We could eventually sum all of these probabilities and we would have a probability distribution. This probability distribution is often called the hazard function. As Allison (1984) states, the fundamental concept in duration models is that the hazard is the outcome that is modelled. This might not at first be obvious and indeed some years ago Sir David Cox commented that a less-appealing aspect of the Cox model is the difficulty of forming a direct physical interpretation of the hazard (Reid, 1994).

We will now move to a short example using some duration data to illustrate the main concepts associated with duration models. We will include some illustrative examples using the software package Stata, which will be discussed further in Chapter 7.

An English city-based college has a computing skills program for women who are unemployed. They collect data in order to evaluate the program. The individual student's enrolment ends when they pass an online test. In particular the college principal is an advocate of massive open online courses (MOOCs) so the college randomizes one group of participants to a course taught by standard methods and another group to the new MOOC. At the beginning of the study 628 women were enrolled on the program. By the end of the study 508 women had passed the test and 120 were right censored (because they had not passed by the end of the study).

A Stata codebook for the data is provided in Figure 5. The dataset includes some additional variables such as the woman's age at enrolment, the number of previous jobs she has had, which of the two college campuses she was inducted at and her educational level. The woman's

Variable	Obs	Unique	Mean	Min	Max	Label
id	628	628	314.5	1	628	student id
time	628	338	234.7038	2	1172	number of days until test passed
test	628	2	.8089172	0	1	test passed (or censored)
age	623	31	32.36918	20	56	age at enrolment
no_jobs	611	28	4.574468	0	40	number of previous jobs
mooc	628	2	.4904459	0	1	taught by massive open online course
campus	628	2	.2929936	0	1	college campus
quals1	628	2	.4601911	0	1	no qualifications
quals2	628	2	.1815287	0	1	lower qualifications (below A'level)
quals3	628	2	.3582803	0	1	higher qualifications(above A'level)

Figure 5 Stata output: Compact codebook for the college skills program dataset

educational level is measured by three dummy variables that take the value of 0 or 1.

The overall mean number of days that the women were enrolled was 235. The mean number of days enrolled for the women who passed the test was 154. The mean number of days enrolled for the women who had not passed the test by the end of the study was 576.

It is important to stress that the duration analysis that is presented below will assess the relative influence that a set of factors have upon how quickly the college students passed the online test. This is a substantively different emphasis to exploring the influences on the 'prevalence' or chance of a wōman passing the online test. This is a subtle but important point to consider because it is easy for data analysts to misleadingly express their modelling results in terms of general prevalence, rather than in terms of effects on durations.

The start of a duration analysis in Stata requires that you declare that survival time data are being analysed using the *stset* command

> *stset time, failure(test)*

The first part of the command declares which variable measures time (which in our example is helpfully called *time*). The second part of the command declares which variable denotes the event. Unfortunately, for historical reasons the 'event' is called a 'failure'. In our example the 'failure' is passing the online test! In other examples where the outcome is death or a light bulb burning out, it is easier to think of the event as a failure.

It is possible to get an overall description of the duration data using Stata's *stdes* command:

> *stdes*

The output is reported in Figure 6. At the beginning of the study the risk set contains all 628 of the women in the study. When a woman passes the test she leaves the risk set and cannot re-enter it. The minimum time before a woman passed the test was 2 days and the maximum time on the program was 1,172 days. The median time on the program was 166 days. Once again an unhelpful terminology features in the output. In our example the 'time at risk' is the period that the woman is at risk of passing the test.

A descriptive graph called a Kaplan-Meier plot is useful for summarizing overall distributions of the time variable. These curves are sometimes called survival curves or survivor functions, and they illustrate the pattern and timing of individuals 'leaving the risk set' (i.e. passing the test). The survivor functions for both women taught by standard methods and women taught using the new MOOC are plotted in Figure 7. The curves appear to indicate that women taught by standard methods leave the

```
        failure _d:  test
  analysis time _t:  time

                               |-------------- per subject --------------|
Category                total       mean       min      median        max
-------------------------------------------------------------------------
no. of subjects           628
no. of records            628          1         1           1          1

(first) entry time                     0         0           0          0
(final) exit time              234.7038         2         166       1172

subjects with gap           0
time on gap if gap          0
time at risk           147394  234.7038         2         166       1172

failures                  508  .8089172         0           1          1
-------------------------------------------------------------------------
```

Figure 6 Stata output: *stdes* command for the college skills program data

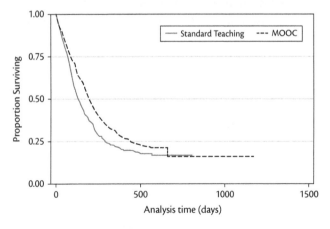

Figure 7 Stata output: Kaplan-Meier plot of time to passing the test by teaching methods (college skills program data)

risk set (i.e. pass the online test) sooner than their counterparts who are taught using the new MOOC.

We can formally test the difference in the *survivor functions* of the women taught by standard teaching methods and the women taught by the new MOOC using the following Stata syntax:

sts test mooc, logrank

The results of the test of the equality of survivor functions are reported in Figure 8. The observed number of passes within the observation window for the women who were taught by standard methods was 265, which was higher than the expected number 236. By contrast the observed number of passes for women taught using the new MOOC was 243, which was lower than the expected number 272. The null hypothesis states that there is no structured or systematic difference between the survivor curves for the women taught by standard methods and the women taught using the new MOOC. By default Stata performs a log-rank test (see Mantel and Haenszel, 1959). We can reject the null hypothesis since $p < 0.01$. There are a number of alternative tests which could be computed using Stata, for example the Wilcoxon (Breslow-Gehan) test (Breslow, 1970; Gehan, 1965). In practice there is usually little difference between the results of these tests (see Lee and Wang, 2003).

We now move on to estimating the Cox regression model, which is a standard approach for modelling durations. We include age at

```
            failure _d:  test
      analysis time _t:  time

  Log-rank test for equality of survivor functions

           |    Events           Events
    mooc   |  observed         expected
  ---------+----------------------------
    0      |     265            235.80
    1      |     243            272.20
  ---------+----------------------------
    Total  |     508            508.00

             chi2(1) =       6.80
             Pr>chi2 =     0.0091
```

Figure 8 Stata output: Log-rank test for equality of survivor functions

enrolment, number of previous jobs, type of teaching method, college campus and previous education. The Cox model is estimated using the following Stata syntax:

stcox age no_jobs mooc campus quals2 quals3, nohr

In this syntax all of the variables are explanatory (i.e. things that might influence differences in durations). The outcome variable is the 'hazard' of passing the test, which is related to the duration, and it is already known to Stata because it has been declared in the *stset* specification and therefore does not need to be explicitly identified in the Stata syntax for estimating this model. Cox regression models can be thought of as another type of statistical model that falls under the generalized linear model (glm) umbrella, where the model assesses how multiple explanatory variables may influence variations in an outcome (see Nelder and Wedderburn, 1972).

The output for the Cox regression model is reported in Figure 9. The first lines of the output report that the failure is measured by the variable *test* and the analysis time (i.e. the duration) is measured by the variable *time*.

```
        failure _d:  test
   analysis time _t:  time

Iteration 0:   log likelihood = -2868.555
Iteration 1:   log likelihood = -2851.6989
Iteration 2:   log likelihood = -2851.0884
Iteration 3:   log likelihood = -2851.0863
Refining estimates:
Iteration 0:   log likelihood = -2851.0863

Cox regression -- Breslow method for ties

No. of subjects =        610          Number of obs    =         610
No. of failures =        495
Time at risk    =     142994
                                      LR chi2(6)       =       34.94
Log likelihood  =   -2851.0863        Prob > chi2      =      0.0000

------------------------------------------------------------------------------
     _t |      Coef.   Std. Err.      z    P>|z|     [95% Conf. Interval]
------------------------------------------------------------------------------
    age | -.0237543   .0075611    -3.14   0.002    -.0385737   -.0089349
 no_jobs |  .034745    .0077538     4.48   0.000     .0195478    .0499422
   mooc | -.2540169   .091005     -2.79   0.005    -.4323834   -.0756504
 campus | -.1723881   .1020981    -1.69   0.091    -.3724966    .0277205
 quals2 |  .2467753   .1227597     2.01   0.044     .0061706    .4873799
 quals3 |   .125668   .1030729     1.22   0.223    -.0763513    .3276873
------------------------------------------------------------------------------
```

Figure 9 Stata output: Cox regression model time to passing the test (college skills program data)

The next block of output reports the iterative steps that are undertaken to estimate the final model. The Cox proportional-hazards likelihood is a particularly difficult function to estimate numerically so the software places extra effort into ensuring appropriate precision, which is why Stata reports that it is 'refining estimates'.

The output reports that the 'Breslow method for ties' is used. If time could be measured on a true continuous scale then no observations would leave the risk set at the same time. In reality, because of the resolution or scale on which we measure time, there may be observations that simultaneously leave the risk set (i.e. they are tied). This affects the size of the risk set because we do not know who left first. Several methods have been proposed for addressing this problem and the default approach in Stata is the Breslow method (see Breslow, 1974). Stata reports that there are 610 women in the analysis and 495 passed the test (i.e. were failures). The total time at risk was 142,994 days. The log likelihood of the current model can be converted into a deviance (i.e. $-2 *$ log likelihood). The difference between the deviance of the null model and the deviance of the current model is reported as the likelihood ratio chi-square (LR chi^2). This can be calculated manually in Stata:

display $(-2*e(ll\_0)) - (-2*e(ll))$

The LR chi^2 is 34.94 at 6 degrees of freedom (i.e. 1 degree of freedom for each explanatory variable in the model), and it is significant ($p < 0.01$). The LR chi^2 value can be considered to be analogous to the *F* test in a standard linear regression model.

The next panel of the output can be interpreted in a similar fashion to a *logit* model. Coefficients for each explanatory variable are reported on the logit scale along with their standard errors and a z test (which is the ratio of the estimate and its standard error). A *p* value for the estimate is reported and a 95 per cent confidence interval is constructed. The coefficients can be considered as the effect on the log of the hazard (Allison, 1984).

The overall message from the results in Figure 9 is that the age at enrolment, the number of previous jobs and the type of teaching method are all significant. The negative coefficients for age and for being taught by an MOOC suggest that on average they are associated with a lower hazard of passing the test (i.e. a longer duration until completion). A higher number of jobs is associated on average with a higher hazard of passing the test (i.e. quicker completion). The effects of the college campus are not significant. The effects of previous education are less obvious. We can formally test the overall (or global) significance of qualifications in this model using the following Stata syntax:

> *test quals2 quals3*

The chi-square test of previous education in the Cox model that is reported in Figure 10 is not significant (p = 0.11). This result can also be derived by comparing the difference between deviance (i.e. −2* log likelihood) for the model reported in Figure 9 with the deviance of a model with the previous education measures excluded.

```
( 1)   quals2 = 0
( 2)   quals3 = 0

       chi2(  2) =    4.36
       Prob > chi2 =  0.1130
```

Figure 10 Stata output: Test of the effects of previous education in Cox regression model of time to passing the test (college skills program data)

```
        failure _d:  test
  analysis time _t:  time

Iteration 0:   log likelihood = -2868.555
Iteration 1:   log likelihood = -2855.3635
Iteration 2:   log likelihood = -2854.6762
Iteration 3:   log likelihood = -2854.6735
Refining estimates:
Iteration 0:   log likelihood = -2854.6735

Cox regression -- Breslow method for ties

No. of subjects =        610              Number of obs   =        610
No. of failures =        495
Time at risk    =     142994
                                          LR chi2(3)      =      27.76
Log likelihood  =  -2854.6735             Prob > chi2     =     0.0000

------------------------------------------------------------------------------
       _t | Haz. Ratio   Std. Err.      z    P>|z|     [95% Conf. Interval]
------------------------------------------------------------------------------
      age |   .9794475    .0072674    -2.80   0.005     .9653067    .9937955
  no_jobs |   1.036128    .0078949     4.66   0.000     1.020769    1.051718
     mooc |   .7940896    .0716076    -2.56   0.011     .6654445    .9476047
------------------------------------------------------------------------------
```

Figure 11 Stata output: Hazard ratios Cox regression model time to passing the test (college skills program data)

A more suitable model might therefore only include age at enrolment, number of previous jobs and method of teaching.

Some data analysts prefer to estimate the Cox regression model and display estimates as *hazard ratios* (which can be thought of as odds). The following Stata syntax omits the option *nohr* (i.e. 'no hazard ratio'):

> *stcox age no_jobs mooc*

Conceptually the hazard of passing the test at time *t* for the women who were taught by the new MOOC was (1 − 0.79) x 100 = 21 per cent lower (*ceteris paribus*). Or expressed another way the women who were taught by the standard methods passed the test sooner than the women who were taught by the new MOOC. Conceptually the hazard of passing the test at time *t* increased (*ceteris paribus*) by 3.6 per cent for each one unit increase in a woman's number of previous jobs (i.e. (1.036 − 1) x 100 = 3.6 per cent). In some research areas the effect of an explanatory variable in a Cox model is described as a 'relative risk'.

One way to quantify these effects is to plot the survival functions to illustrate comparisons. Figure 12 shows the survival functions for women who were aged 30 and had 5 previous jobs. The survival function for

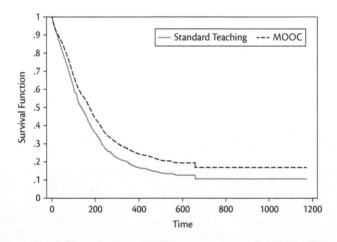

Figure 12 Stata output: Time to passing the test – survival functions comparing women aged 30 with 5 previous jobs by teaching methods (college skills program data)

women taught by the MOOC indicates that it generally takes them longer to leave the risk set (i.e. pass the test).

In the current model we have made no explicit consideration about the shape of the hazard function. An assumption of the Cox model is that the hazards are proportional, that is, that the effect of a given covariate does not change over time (Persson, 2002). In the statistical literature this is sometimes referred to as the 'proportional hazards assumption'. There are several methods for verifying that a model satisfies the assumption of proportionality. One method is to include time-dependent covariates in the model. The options *tvc* and *texp* are available in Stata. An alternative method for assessing the proportionality assumption is to test Schoenfeld residuals (Grambsch and Therneau, 1994). The test can be undertaken in Stata using the following syntax after the *stcox* model has been estimated:

  estat phtest, detail

Parametric duration models

The Cox regression model estimates the baseline survivor function without any reference to a theoretical distribution (Hamilton, 2012). This is why in the statistical literature the model is sometimes referred to as a 'semi-parametric' model. In practice, this means that models can be estimated without the researcher knowing (or having to assume) an appropriate distribution, which is an attractive feature of the model for empirical research. There are a number of 'parametric' versions of the model, which are based on the idea that the survival times follow a known distribution. These models have the same general form as the Cox model but define the baseline hazard differently. A useful way to conceptualize parametric functions of durations is to consider them as representing the accumulation of something. This accumulation begins at $t = 0$ and therefore we can assume that the measurement is 0 at $t = 0$. For example, primary smoking-related lung damage begins when the person starts smoking cigarettes. The general methodological advice is that how the accumulation process works should inform the choice of parametric function used in the modelling framework.

A range of parametric duration models can be estimated using Stata's *streg* command. Here we will mention only two distributions. The first is the exponential distribution which specifies a constant hazard. The under-lying assumption is that events are independent and are not influenced by time. Therefore, in an analysis, individuals would be no more likely to experience the event later in the study than they were earlier in the study. This distribution is suitable if there is no 'ageing' effect in the social process that is being studied. For many social science research questions this is an unrealistic assumption. The second distribution is the Weibull distribution, which does not require failure rates to be constant over time and allows them to smoothly increase or decrease.

Zorn (2000) provides an advanced, but accessible, account of the potential challenges associated with duration dependence in the context of social science research. When there are several possible parametric models that could be used for an analysis, thought should be placed into which model is most appropriate. A sensible strategy for evaluating alter-native models is to use a measure such as the Akaike Information Criterion (AIC) (see Akaike, 1974).

Competing risk models

The techniques that have been outlined above have all involved the analysis of a simple single event. We can easily envisage social science examples where a process ends with more than one possible outcome. Imagine a study of young people claiming unemployment benefits. The spell is unemployment and it may be ended by one of several substan-tively interesting alternative outcomes, for example gaining a full-time job, gaining a part-time job, entering a training scheme, returning to education or leaving the labour market. The 'competing-risks model' extends the Cox model to handle multiple outcomes (see Fine and Gray, 1999). We can think of these multiple outcomes as 'risks' of things that compete to end the respondent's spell (i.e. time in the initial state).

For many social science analyses where the phenomenon of interest is characterized by more than two states the competing-risks model may be more suitable than a simpler Cox model. The competing-risks model can be estimated in Stata using the *stcrreg* command. We do not present a competing-risks example as it is sufficiently similar to the Cox model. A limitation of the competing-risks model is that the relative hazards of different risks can be quite complicated to describe appropriately. When there are a number of different competing risks, the identification of model parameters can be difficult. In practice researchers often choose to strategically limit the number of different competing risks that they explore within one model. The drawback is that this can sometimes lead to an inappropriate simplification of the characteristics of more complex social processes.

Discrete-time models

Discrete-time models are an alternative approach to duration data analysis and are also widely used in the social sciences. In discrete-time duration data the spell is partitioned into a number of different components that are aligned to distinctive or 'discrete' time periods. An essential property of the model used for the analysis of discrete time is the discrete hazard. This is the conditional probability that an individual will experience an event during the current discrete-time period, given that they have not previously experienced it. Singer and Willett (2003) advocate discrete-time approaches as a convenient alternative to continuous-time approaches and they argue that the simplicity of discrete-time approaches makes them an ideal entrée into the analysis of duration data. Stata does not have a suite of in-built commands for discrete-time models. This is because the models can be easily estimated using standard techniques.

The techniques and methods that have been outlined so far in this chapter use data that are recorded in continuous time. Continuous-time data are usually organized in a 'wide format' (this is often known as a 'person-time' dataset). In this format each row of the data represents a respondent or unit in the study. Discrete-time analysis requires what is sometimes referred to as a 'person-period' dataset. This is a 'long format' dataset where each row represents a 'person' at a given discrete-time period. For example, a dataset might contain several rows per person, one for each annual wave of a household panel survey. In Chapter 7 we outline the formats of 'long' and 'wide' datasets.

Like most data enabling tasks there are a number of possible approaches to organizing discrete-time data. The data need to be 'expanded' from a (continuous) 'person-time' format to a (discrete) 'person-period' format (i.e. from 'wide' to 'long' format). There are a number of facilities to do this, but we advocate using the Stata command *prsnperd*, which is a utility for creating discrete-time datasets from continuous-time data, although some researchers prefer Stata's *stsplit* command.

The package *dthaz* provides tools for discrete-time analysis and must first be downloaded using the syntax *net install dthaz* from http://www.alexisdinno.com/stata.

Once the data are in the person-period format, it is possible to estimate a discrete-time model using standard cross-sectional modelling techniques, for example a logistic regression model.

Discrete-time duration data analysis has long been recognized as a useful alternative means of exploring durations in the social sciences (Tuma, 1982). Although the format imposes some granularity upon the measure of duration, it does mean that standard models can be used to analyse the data. The techniques have been successfully applied in many studies. For example, Henley (1998) estimated single and competing risk discrete-time duration models of residence duration using the BHPS. Ermisch and Francesconi (2000) used discrete-time models to analyse cohabitation using BHPS. Berrington and Diamond (2000a) used discrete-time competing-risks models to analyse first partnerships in the NCDS.

Conclusions

Duration models are useful tools when the focus of the research question is the time to an event, and the event is a relatively crisp change between states. Because of the general appeal of analysing time to an event, duration models have been applied in areas as diverse as medicine, engineering, economics and sociology. The Cox model provides a robust and flexible starting point and Therneau (1997) states that it has become the workhorse of duration analyses with censored data.

The distinction between analysis in continuous-time frameworks and discrete-time frameworks is sometimes highlighted. Allison (2010) provides the following succinct, and in our view cogent, recommendations. First, if the exact time at which an event occurs is known then it is appropriate to use a continuous-time approach. Second, if only the month or the year of the event is recorded, discrete-time methods are better suited. Third, a very good indication of the need for discrete-time methods is the presence of a large number of ties (e.g. where two or more individuals experience an event at the same recorded time). Fourth, in some circumstances time is genuinely discrete, in the sense that events can occur only at certain discrete points in time.

Many different duration models can be estimated. The software Stata supports many options using its *st* suite (*st* stands for survival times). Blosfeld, Golsch and Rohwer (2007), Cleves (2016) and Royston and Lambert (2011) provide extensive and informative sources on using the *st* suite. The methods outlined in this chapter can be extended and more complex modelling approaches are available in both continuous-time and discrete-time frameworks. For example, multiple failure-time data, or multivariate survival data as it is alternatively known, is a natural extension to the techniques that have been outlined above. These more advanced techniques are suitable for the analysis of data from time-to-occurrence studies when two or more events occur for the same subject. Duration models can also be extended to circumstances where the durations for different units are related to each other, for example family members or classmates. In these studies, failure times are correlated within clusters of cases, violating the assumption of independence required in standard survival analysis (see Rabe-Hesketh and Skrondal, 2012). An outline of multiple-spell discrete-time analysis methods is provided by Willett and Singer (1995), and Steele, Goldstein and Browne (2004) document and apply a general multilevel multistate competing-risks model for event history data.

The central focus upon how long individuals remain in a certain state until an explicit event takes place means that the analysis of duration data is a more specific and narrowly defined approach in comparison to other methods of longitudinal data analysis. In the next chapter we turn our attention to more general strategies for analysing repeated contacts data.

5 The analysis of repeated contacts data

....

Introduction

In this chapter we turn our attention to the analysis of repeated contacts social science data. In the pages below we focus upon the analytical aspects of working with panel data and include some specific examples that use the Stata software for modelling panel data. The data analysis techniques that will be introduced in this chapter generally require the quantitative longitudinal dataset to be in 'long format' (which is outlined further in Chapter 7). In a 'long format' dataset each row of the dataset will be an individual (i) at a specific time point (t). In practice a substantial amount of effort is often required to suitably enable repeated contacts data before analysis begins.

Approaches to analysing panel data: Part 1

A simple statistical model that can be estimated with panel data is the pooled cross-sectional model. As the name suggests, all of the observations for each individual in the panel are pooled together and they are analysed using the standard statistical model that would be used for a cross-sectional analysis. In the case of a continuous outcome Y, a linear regression model estimated using Ordinary Least Squares (OLS) would be used to analyse the pooled data from the panel.

Estimating a pooled cross-sectional model is a good place to begin, and it is useful in the exploratory phase of the data analysis process. Results from a pooled cross-sectional model will provide some initial information on the relationships between the explanatory variables and the outcome variable. The overall limitation of the pooled cross-sectional model is that it assumes that each observation (i.e. row within a long format dataset) is independent of other observations. When analysing panel data we know that individual respondents contribute many times to the data, usually once per 'wave' for many waves. In a long format panel dataset a respondent will contribute multiple rows of data. Therefore, pooling all of the data and analysing them together violates the standard regression modelling assumption that each observation is independent.

In practice, when used to analyse panel datasets the pooled cross-sectional model tends to estimate standard errors that are too small. The model does not recognize that there are multiple contributions of data from the same individuals, and therefore, it estimates results as if there were many individuals who shared the same characteristics. This impacts upon the estimate of measures such as variances and standard errors.

A practical strategy for improving upon the simple pooled cross-sectional model is to estimate the model with robust standard errors. Robust standard errors are sometimes known as Huber/White sandwich estimates of variance (see White, 1984; Huber, 1967). The use of robust standard errors helps to correct results from pooled cross-sectional models, where the non-independence of observations assumption is violated. Stata calculates robust standard errors for a wide variety of regression models (see Rogers, 1994, for a discussion of the formula and methods used in this procedure within Stata). In practice the robust standard errors will most often be larger than the uncorrected standard errors that are produced by a standard pooled cross-sectional model.

Another approach to analysing panel data is the analysis of changes or differences in scores (see Allison, 1990). This is a model of the change in a score between two time points, for example two waves of a survey. This model can be illustrated with a simple example. A sample of social science students might be given a statistics test at the start of an academic term and then be re-tested at the end of the term. A regression model of the change in their scores would then be estimated. In the case of a continuous outcome measure that is collected at two different time points (t_1 and t_2), in a change score model the outcome will be the difference $Y_{t2} - Y_{t1}$. It is easy to see why this approach is sometimes called a 'first difference' model. An example of using this approach to analyse change in attitudes between two waves of BHPS is provided in Berrington, Smith and Sturgis (2006).

Implementations of change score models are often limited to comparisons of scores between two discrete time points (Finkel, 1995). Alternative change scores can be derived, such as calculating changes over different or

even multiple time periods. Dalecki and Willits (1991) provide an evaluation of three approaches to analysing changes in scores. In some scenarios,
analysing change scores is thought to exacerbate the unreliability of the
measures concerned. This is because the emphasis is now on studying the
difference between two scores, both of which might be measured with
error (see Taris, 2000). Change score models can also be thought of as
simpler versions of other techniques for analysing repeated contacts data,
for example 'differences in differences' techniques, which are popular
within economics (see Angrist and Pischke, 2009), and the 'dynamic panel
model', which we will cover later in this chapter (see Liker et al., 1985).

A different approach to analysing a panel of repeated measures is to
use only mean information for each individual respondent. This is often
referred to as a 'between effects' approach. In practice, this involves
collapsing the long format dataset into a small dataset which contains
one single row for each respondent. The new rows of data are a set of
individual-specific averages.

Figure 13 is a snapshot of a long format panel dataset for a single
respondent (*id*== 3) for three waves of a panel study (1968, 1969 and 1970).
There is one outcome variable *ln_wage*, which is the log of weekly wages
(adjusted for inflation). There are two explanatory variables: *hour*, which is
the number of hours per week normally worked in the respondent's main
job, and *age*, which is the respondent's age at the time of the survey.

Figure 14 is a snapshot of data for respondent *id*==3 after the data for
the three waves have been collapsed. The collapsed dataset now contains
only a single row of data for the respondent (*id*==3). The outcome variable
is now the mean of the log of weekly wages (adjusted for inflation). The

id	year	age	hours	ln_wage
3	68	22	40	1.49
3	69	23	40	1.70
3	70	24	40	1.45

id: personal identification number
year: year of the survey
age: respondent's age in years
hours: number of hours per week normally worked in main job
ln_wage: log of weekly wages (adjusted for inflation)

Figure 13 Snapshot of long format panel dataset

id	year $\bar{x}$	age $\bar{x}$	hours $\bar{x}$	ln_wage $\bar{x}$
3	69	23	40	1.55

id: personal identification number
year $\bar{x}$: mean year of the survey
age $\bar{x}$: mean of respondent's age in years
hours $\bar{x}$: mean number of hours per week normally worked in main job
ln_wage $\bar{x}$: mean log of weekly wages (adjusted for inflation)

Figure 14 Snapshot of a collapsed dataset of mean values of variables (in Figure 13)

two explanatory variables are now mean hours per week normally worked in the respondent's main job and their mean age across the three waves of the survey.

The between effects approach estimates a standard cross-sectional model on these data. For example, consider a regression model with the outcome variable Y (the mean of the log of weekly wages adjusted for inflation), estimated with the two explanatory variables (the mean hours per week normally worked in the respondent's main job and the respondent's mean age across the three waves of the survey). Because now there is only one row of data per respondent the problem of non-independence of observations in the original ('long format') panel data is sidestepped.

The between effects approach is appealing because it is a relatively simple method to comprehend and it relies on standard cross-sectional methods of analysis. As we will see below a between effects model can easily be estimated using Stata. In some analyses the mean values of an individual's variables might provide a suitable summary and therefore be appropriate for answering the particular research question. The between effects approach clearly neglects the patterns of change over time within subjects, and for this reason it might not be considered the most useful technique, but it does play a part in more comprehensive approaches to the analysis of panel data.

Approaches to analysing panel data: Part 2

A range of statistical models often known as panel regression models provide extensions to the approaches in Part 1. The panel regression model takes into account the multiple contributions that an individual respondent makes to the dataset, and it provides additional control for the effects of residual heterogeneity. The two most widely used models for analysing panel data are usually referred to as the 'fixed effects' panel model and the 'random effects' panel model.

There is a reasonable degree of confusion surrounding these seemingly innocuous labels. This is partly because different academic disciplines and research areas use alternative terminologies and definitions. Gelman (2005) provides an insightful review that highlights the considerable confusion in the use of these terms. A number of different styles of notation are used to describe the fixed and random effects panel models, which is partly historical and once again partly due to alternative conventions in different research areas. In the coming passage we will outline the main features of the fixed effects panel model and the random effects panel model before describing how they are applied in quantitative longitudinal data analysis. Figure 15 provides a summary of features of the fixed effects panel model.

One way to conceptualize how the fixed effect panel model is estimated is to consider it as a standard cross-sectional regression model with the addition of a dummy variable being included for every respondent in the dataset except for one (i.e. $n - 1$ dummy variables are added to the model). This is why the fixed effects panel model is sometimes referred to as the least squares dummy variable (LSDV) approach (see Cameron and Trivedi, 2010). The mechanism behind this approach can be demonstrated graphically. Figure 16 shows a set of repeated observations for a simple panel of four respondents. Looking at the graph it is clear that the standard cross-sectional regression line (the dashed line) is a poor

---

The fixed effects panel model

Concentrates on change over time within an individual's responses

Can include explanatory variables that, for the individual respondent, change over time (e.g. age, monthly income and body mass index)

In general cannot include explanatory variables that, for the individual respondent, are time-constant (e.g. town of birth, birth weight, father's occupation when respondent was aged 14)

Has the potentially attractive property of providing robust estimates when observed explanatory variables are correlated with the unobserved effects

---

Figure 15 A summary of the features of the fixed effects panel model

summary of the data. A standard regression line would be an unsuitable approach for summarizing individual-level change over time such as growth or development. If, however, we added a dummy variable for each of the individual respondents, we would have an intercept that is unique

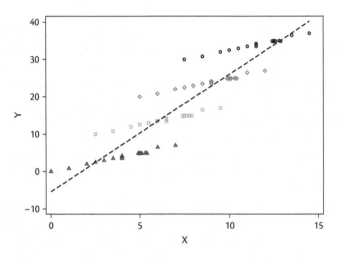

Figure 16 Graph of a simple set of panel data

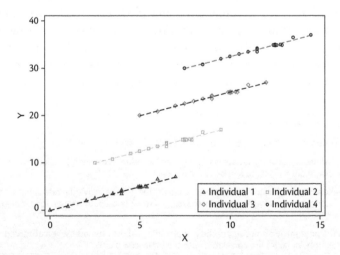

Figure 17 Graph of a simple set of panel data with constant slopes but individual intercepts

for each individual. The regression line would then summarize patterns of change within individuals, and this is illustrated in Figure 17.

The fixed effects panel model can also be thought of as an extension of the change score approach. This is because the underlying calculations of the fixed effects panel model are based on differencing. It is easy to see why variables that are fixed in time cannot usually be incorporated into analyses using this model. For example, if a fixed-in-time variable such as gender (*female==1*) is the same for an individual in all 10 waves of a panel dataset, then its influence on within-person change between waves cannot easily be estimated.

Figure 18 provides a summary of features of the random effects model. The random effects panel model shares several similar features to the fixed effects panel model. One of the key practical differences is that it can include explanatory variables that change over time and explanatory variables that are fixed in time. This is an attractive property for many social science research questions. Therefore, the random effects panel model, unlike the fixed effects panel model, does not concentrate solely on change over time for an individual respondent. The random effects panel model also facilitates some analysis of the differences between individual respondents.

A key technical difference between the fixed effects panel model and the random effects panel model is that in the random effects formulation, the individual-specific effect is considered to be drawn from a probability distribution (see Cameron and Trivedi, 2005). This means that the random effects model does not estimate a parameter for each individual respondent, but it does calculate a parameter that summarizes the overall distribution of individual respondents' differences (e.g. a variance estimate for this distribution).

The random effects panel model

Analyses both change within an individual respondent's outcomes, and differences between respondents' outcomes

Can include explanatory variables that, for the individual respondent, change over time (e.g. age, monthly income and body mass index)

Can include explanatory variables that, for the individual respondent, are time-constant (e.g. town of birth, birth weight, father's occupation when respondent was aged 14)

Makes the assumption that observed explanatory variables are not correlated with the unobserved effects

---

Figure 18 A summary of the features of the random effects panel model

Pooled Cross-Sectional Regression Model

(1) $Y_{it} = \beta_0 + \beta_1 X_{1it} + ... + \beta_k X_{kit} + \varepsilon_{it}$

Fixed Effects Panel Regression Model

(2) $Y_{it} = \beta_0 + \lambda_i + \beta_1 X_{1it} + ... + \beta_k X_{kit} + \varepsilon_{it}$

Random Effects Panel Regression Model ('random intercepts' version)

(3) $Y_{it} = \beta_0 + + \beta_1 X_{1it} + ... + \beta_k X_{kit} + \upsilon_i + \varepsilon_{it}$

Figure 19 Simple notation for a pooled cross-sectional model, a fixed effects panel model and a random effects panel model

One important aspect of the random effects panel model, which is widely highlighted in economics but is sometimes downplayed in other disciplines, is the assumption that the observed explanatory variables are not correlated with the unobserved effects. This assumption is often unrealistic and we will return to this issue later.

At this point it might be useful to understand a little about the construction of the panel models and their notation. Equation (1) in Figure 19 is the pooled cross-sectional regression model. This model includes *i* and *t* subscripts for records. Equation (2) in Figure 19 represents the fixed effects panel regression model. It includes an important additional parameter, λ_i, which can be considered as an individual effect that is constant over time (which is why it has the *i* subscript but not a *t* subscript). Putting this information together we should now be able to see how we can arrive at different intercepts for each respondent in the panel as depicted in Figure 17. In Figure 17 the single line that is shown going through each individual's observations is the product of an overall line that is shifted up or down according to the value of the individual-specific intercept.

Equation (3) in Figure 19 shows a third formulation, which is a common notation for the random effects panel model.[1] At first sight the random

_____

1 We note that this is the 'random intercepts' version of the random effects model, and this is because the random effects model is also sometimes extended into what is often called a 'random coefficients' model. Typically in a random coefficients model, the individual-specific error term can also be modelled as a function of other explanatory variables.

effects and fixed effects specifications look very similar, because the only addition to the pooled cross-sectional model is a new term that represents a distinctive value relating to each individual respondent. An important difference between the fixed effects panel model and the random effects panel model is that in the latter, this term is treated as part of the error variance (i.e. as part of the random errors) and its values are not estimated as part of the model.[2] This contrasts with the fixed effects model where the λ_i is directly estimated alongside the estimates of other model coefficients. In the notation for the random effects panel model, there are two different components to the error variance. This is why the term 'variance components model' is used in some areas of statistics to describe this model.

Technical accounts of the fixed and random effects panel models are provided in Baltagi (2008), Wooldridge (2010), Greene (2012a) and Hsiao (2014). Within the social sciences, random effects models are widely used for the analysis of other forms of clustered data aside from panel datasets. The phrase 'multilevel model' is frequently used to denote random effects models applied to both panel and non-panel data (e.g. see Goldstein, 2011).

Comparing different panel models: Example 1

The estimation mechanisms behind the fixed effects panel model and the random effects panel model are often initially nebulous for social science researchers (especially for those whose interests are substantive rather than methodological). Through the use of a 'toy' panel dataset, we will now illustrate some of the underlying ideas and the links and differences between these two models.

The 'toy' panel dataset consists of 32 observations that come from 8 individuals. Each individual is measured at 4 different waves. The outcome variable Y is continuous and takes on values from 1 to 11, with a mean of

---

2 In a fuller algebraic representation of the models, the difference between the random effects and fixed effects models might be depicted by explicitly stating the assumptions about the error distribution for the random error term, υ_i.

5.38 and a standard deviation of .49. There are two explanatory measures. The first is *gender*, and there are 4 males and 4 females. In this example *gender* is time constant and none of the respondents change their value for gender during the life of the panel. The second explanatory variable is an indicator of *wave*, which is represented by three dummy variables which take on the value of 0 or 1.

A useful way of considering the two explanatory variables is that the first is a 'between-respondents' measure and the second is a 'within-respondents' measure. A summary of these measures is provided in Figure 20.

The first model that could be estimated is a standard cross-sectional regression model. To recap, this model is estimated with OLS and is often called a pooled model, because it 'pools' the data for each of the individual respondents. The pooled model is a naïve approach to analysing a panel dataset because it ignores the non-independence of the observations. The pooled model is a regression of 32 independent observations, but we know that there are only 8 respondents and each has contributed an outcome at 4 points in time. The results of the pooled regression model are reported in Figure 21.

The next model that we estimate is the between effects model and the results are reported in Figure 22. As the Stata output reports, the between

```
Variable    Obs    Mean    Min   Max             Label
------------------------------------------------------------------------
   y         32     5.38     1    11             y outcome variable
   id        32     4.50     1     8             id
 female      32      .50     0     1             female
 wave2       32      .25     0     1             wave 2
 wave3       32      .25     0     1             wave 3
 wave4       32      .25     0     1             wave 4
------------------------------------------------------------------------
```

Figure 20 Summary of panel dataset measures

```
------------------------------------------------------------------------
       y |    Coef.   Std. Err.      t    P|t|    [95% Conf. Interval]
---------+--------------------------------------------------------------
  female |     .625   .4187448     1.49   0.147   -.2341934    1.484193
   wave2 |      .75   .5921946     1.27   0.216    -.465083    1.965083
   wave3 |      3.5   .5921946     5.91   0.000    2.284917    4.715083
   wave4 |     6.25   .5921946    10.55   0.000    5.034917    7.465083
   _cons |   2.4375   .4681709     5.21   0.000    1.476893    3.398107
------------------------------------------------------------------------
```

Figure 21 Stata output: Pooled regression model (OLS)

effects model is a regression on group means. In this model there are 8 respondents (unhelpfully referred to as 'groups' in the output) contributing 32 observations. It is worth noting that only a coefficient for the first explanatory variable *female* has been estimated. In this 'toy' example the panel is balanced and each individual makes a contribution to each and every one of the 4 waves of the survey, which means that the explanatory variables relating to the waves of the survey all have exactly the same average values for each individual, and their effects cannot be estimated in the between effects model.

The between effects model can be considered as a regression model using the individual respondent's mean values for their variables. This is easily illustrated if we collapse the dataset into a new dataset containing only the mean values for each of the respondents. If we estimate a regression model with each of the eight individuals' mean of their *X* variables on their mean of *Y*, then we have reconstructed the between effects model. Compare the results in Figure 22 with the results in Figure 23.

The between effects model is clearly drawing on a more limited amount of information than is available within the data. We will see below that the between effects model plays an important role by contributing information to other models, however.

The next model we outline is the fixed effects panel model, which is reported in Figure 24. In this model the first explanatory variable *female* is omitted. This is because the fixed effects model works on the calculation

```
Between regression (regression on group means)    Number of obs    =        32
Group variable: id                                Number of groups =         8

R-sq:                                             Obs per group:
    within  = .                                                min =         4
    between = 0.2500                                            avg =       4.0
    overall = 0.0133                                            max =         4

                                                  F(1,6)           =      2.00
sd(u_i + avg(e_i.))=       .625                   Prob  F          =    0.2070

------------------------------------------------------------------------------
         y |      Coef.   Std. Err.      t    P|t|     [95% Conf. Interval]
-----------+------------------------------------------------------------------
    female |       .625   .4419417     1.41   0.207    -.4563925    1.706392
     wave2 |          0  (omitted)
     wave3 |          0  (omitted)
     wave4 |          0  (omitted)
     _cons |     5.0625      .3125    16.20   0.000     4.29784     5.82716
------------------------------------------------------------------------------
```

Figure 22 Stata output: Between effects regression model

```
note: mean_wave1 omitted because of collinearity
note: mean_wave2 omitted because of collinearity
note: mean_wave3 omitted because of collinearity

      Source |       SS           df       MS        Number of obs   =        8
-------------+----------------------------------     F(1, 6)         =     2.00
       Model |     .78125            1      .78125   Prob > F        =   0.2070
    Residual |    2.34375            6     .390625   R-squared       =   0.2500
-------------+----------------------------------     Adj R-squared   =   0.1250
       Total |      3.125            7  .446428571   Root MSE        =     .625

------------------------------------------------------------------------------
      y_mean |      Coef.   Std. Err.      t    P>|t|     [95% Conf. Interval]
-------------+----------------------------------------------------------------
 mean_female |       .625   .4419417     1.41   0.207    -.4563925    1.706392
  mean_wave1 |          0  (omitted)
  mean_wave2 |          0  (omitted)
  mean_wave3 |          0  (omitted)
       _cons |     5.0625      .3125    16.20   0.000     4.29784     5.82716
------------------------------------------------------------------------------
```

Figure 23 Stata output: Regression model on individual means (manual version of the between effects regression model)

```
Fixed-effects (within) regression              Number of obs    =        32
Group variable: id                             Number of groups =         8

R-sq:                                          Obs per group:
     within  = 0.8722                                        min =         4
     between =      .                                        avg =       4.0
     overall = 0.8259                                        max =         4

                                               F(3,21)          =     47.77
corr(u_i, Xb)  = -0.0000                        Prob  F          =    0.0000

------------------------------------------------------------------------------
           y |      Coef.   Std. Err.      t    P|t|      [95% Conf. Interval]
-------------+----------------------------------------------------------------
      female |          0  (omitted)
       wave2 |        .75   .5824824     1.29   0.212    -.4613384    1.961338
       wave3 |        3.5   .5824824     6.01   0.000     2.288662    4.711338
       wave4 |       6.25   .5824824    10.73   0.000     5.038662    7.461338
       _cons |       2.75   .4118772     6.68   0.000     1.893454    3.606546
-------------+----------------------------------------------------------------
     sigma_u |   .6681531
     sigma_e |  1.1649647
         rho |   .24752475   (fraction of variance due to u_i)
------------------------------------------------------------------------------
F test that all u_i=0: F(7, 21) = 1.32                     Prob  F = 0.2914
```

Figure 24 Stata output: Fixed effects panel model

of differences, and the first explanatory variable *female* is time constant and therefore does not change value for individuals during the lifetime of the panel.

The final model we estimate is the random effects panel model and the results are reported in Figure 25. In this model the first explanatory

```
Random-effects GLS regression              Number of obs     =        32
Group variable: id                         Number of groups  =         8

R-sq:                                      Obs per group:
    within  = 0.8722                                   min =         4
    between = 0.2500                                   avg =       4.0
    overall = 0.8392                                   max =         4

                                           Wald chi2(4)      =    145.32
corr(u_i, X)   = 0 (assumed)               Prob  chi2        =    0.0000

------------------------------------------------------------------------------
         y |     Coef.   Std. Err.      z    P|z|     [95% Conf. Interval]
-----------+------------------------------------------------------------------
    female |     .625    .4419417     1.41   0.157    -.2411899    1.49119
     wave2 |      .75    .5824824     1.29   0.198    -.3916445   1.891644
     wave3 |      3.5    .5824824     6.01   0.000     2.358356   4.641644
     wave4 |     6.25    .5824824    10.73   0.000     5.108356   7.391644
     _cons |   2.4375    .474224      5.14   0.000     1.508038   3.366962
-----------+------------------------------------------------------------------
   sigma_u |  .22658174
   sigma_e |  1.1649647
       rho |  .03645008    (fraction of variance due to u_i)
------------------------------------------------------------------------------
```

Figure 25 Stata output: Random effects panel model

variable *female*, which is 'time constant', is included alongside *wave*, which is a 'time-varying' effect (and is measured by the three dummy variables). The random effects panel model estimates effects for both 'between-respondents' measures and 'within-respondents' measures.

Let us examine the coefficients (or betas) from each of the three models, which are reported in Figure 26. In the random effects model the value of the coefficient for the first explanatory variable *female* is the same as the value of the coefficient in the between effects models. In the random effects model the coefficients for the second explanatory variable *wave*, which is the 'within-respondents' effect (measured by three dummy variables), have the same values as the coefficients in the fixed effects models.

The random effects panel model is using (or borrowing) some information from the fixed effects panel model, at the same time as borrowing some information from the between effects model. This should help to illustrate why econometricians often make oral statements such as 'the random effects panel model is a matrix weighted average of the within effects (fixed effects) and the between effects'.

Finally, we can discover a little more about how the models are interwoven by testing the effects from the random effects model. The results of these tests are reported in Figure 27. For the *female* variable $F = 2$, which is the same as the F value in the between effects model in Figure 22. The F value

	BE b(se)	FE b(se)	RE b(se)
female	0.625	0.000	0.625
	(0.442)	(.)	(0.442)
wave2	0.000	0.750	0.750
	(.)	(0.582)	(0.582)
wave3	0.000	3.500***	3.500***
	(.)	(0.582)	(0.582)
wave4	0.000	6.250***	6.250***
	(.)	(0.582)	(0.582)
_cons	5.063***	2.750***	2.438***
	(0.313)	(0.412)	(0.474)
n	32	32	32

BE: Between Effects Model
FE: Fixed Effects Panel Model
RE: Random Effects Panel Model

Figure 26 Stata output: Coefficients (b) and their standard errors (se) from the between effects model, the fixed effects panel model and the random effects panel model

Variable	F	df
female	2	1
wave1 wave2 wave3	47.77	3

Figure 27 Stata output: Coefficients F tests for the random effects panel model

in the between effects model has 1,6 degrees of freedom. The first number is the model degrees of freedom (or the number of explanatory variables in the model). The second number is the residual degrees of freedom. The total number of degrees of freedom for the model is 7 (n−1). The model degrees of freedom is 1 (there are k = 1 explanatory variables in the model). So there are 6 residual degrees of freedom (7 total degrees of freedom − 1 model degree of freedom).

For the variable *wave*, the 'within-respondents' effect (which is measured by the three dummy variables) $F = 47.77$. This is the same as the value of F in the fixed effects panel model reported in Figure 24. The F value in the fixed effects model has 3,21 degrees of freedom. The first number represents the k=3 explanatory variables in the fixed effects model. The total number of degrees of freedom for the model is 31 (i.e. the number of observations − 1). The model degrees of freedom equals 10; this is 3 (i.e. k explanatory variables) plus 7 (i.e. the number of individual respondents −1). There are 21 residual degrees of freedom (i.e. 31 total degrees of freedom − 10 model degrees of freedom).

In this tidy 'toy' example the models produce congenial results. As we will see later in genuine research examples using real panel data, the results from the models will not necessarily line up as neatly. The computation behind the estimation of the panel models will however follow these underlying principles.

Comparing different panel models: Example 2

In this section we use an extract of data from the BHPS in order to elaborate upon the techniques and the models that have been introduced earlier in the chapter. The extract of data covers the first 10 waves of the BHPS (1991–2001). The panel comprises men aged 25–35 in 1991 and working full-time. They are original members of the BHPS sample, by which we mean they are members of the main BHPS and have not entered the study as part of the territorial booster samples, or the ECHP. The outcome variable of interest is their usual net pay per month (£) in their current job (which has been adjusted for inflation). There are a number of explanatory variables relating to the respondent's occupation, their level of education and their circumstances in childhood.

A compact codebook for the data is reported in Figure 28. The dataset contains the cross-wave person identifier *pid*, an indicator for the wave

```
Variable   Obs Unique      Mean       Min       Max  Label
-------------------------------------------------------------------------------
pid       8414  1325   1.99e+07  1.00e+07  1.07e+08  cross-wave person identifier
wave      8414    10   5.381745         1        10  wave of the BHPS
zhid      8414  8332    5793900   1000381  1.07e+07  household identification number
zpno      8414     7   1.497029         1         7  person number
zdoby     8414     9   1960.982      1957      1965  year of birth
zpaynu2   6098  3898    1050.62  50.14124  9741.704  usual net pay per month(deflated 1991)
zjbhrs    6435    60   40.47677         0        99  no. of hours normally worked per week
zjbcssm   7503   558   34.75936       .56     90.32  cambridge scale males: present job
pacssm    6829   347   30.13144       .56     85.04  cambridge scale males: father's job
graduate  7926     2   .1683068         0         1  graduates (based on wqfachi)
zregage   8414    19   9.177324         0        18  age at interview-25
-------------------------------------------------------------------------------
```

Figure 28 Stata compact codebook for the BHPS extract of male full-time workers aged 25–35 waves 1–10

of the BHPS *wave*, a household identification number *zhid* and a linking variable *zpno* that helps to identify which person in the BHPS household the respondent is. The dataset also includes the respondent's year of birth *zdoby*. The outcome variable *zpaynu2* measures the respondent's usual net pay per month (£) and has been adjusted for inflation.[3] The number of hours normally worked per week in the respondent's main job is measured by the variable *zjbhrs*. The Cambridge Scale Score (male) of the respondent's present occupation is recorded by the variable *zjbcssm* (see Prandy, 1990). The Cambridge Scale Score (male) of the respondent's father's occupation when the respondent was aged 14 is recorded by the variable *pacssm*. A simple measure of the respondent's level of education is recorded in the dummy indicator *graduate*. The respondent's age at the time of the interview (age in years – 25) is recorded in the variable *zregage*.

The measures that will be included in the analyses are summarized in Figure 29. The first step in the analysis is the estimation of a pooled cross-sectional model. The pooled cross-sectional model is estimated using OLS with the following Stata syntax:

reg zpaynu2 zjbhr zjbcssm pacssm graduate zregage i.wave

Variable	Obs	Mean	Std. Dev.	Min	Max
pid	8,414	19930791	15556858	10004491	107127261
wave	8,414	5.381745	2.883981	1	10
zhid	8,414	5793900	2815185	1000381	10677259
zpno	8,414	1.497029	.8550912	1	7
zdoby	8,414	1960.982	2.607062	1957	1965
zpaynu2	6,098	1050.62	488.2907	50.14124	9741.704
zjbhrs	6,435	40.47677	7.895388	0	99
zjbcssm	7,503	34.75936	19.10313	.56	90.32
pacssm	6,829	30.13144	19.00808	.56	85.04
graduate	7,926	.1683068	.3741621	0	1
zregage	8,414	9.177324	3.854532	0	18

Figure 29 Stata summary for the BHPS extract of male full-time workers aged 25–35 waves 1–10

---

3 One convention is to analyse the log of income rather than the income itself, due to the positive skew of income measures. In this example we use the raw values because students have stated that it is easier to understand.

The results of the pooled cross-sectional model are reported in Figure 30. The pooled cross-sectional model is a good starting point for the analyses. A synoptic assessment of the results reported in Figure 30 indicates that the number of hours normally worked per week in the respondent's main job, the Cambridge Scale Scores for their own main job and their father's job when they were aged 14, being a graduate and their age at interview, all have a significant effect on *zpaynu2* (their usual net pay per month in £ adjusted for inflation). To a lesser extent the specific wave of the survey can also be important.

At this stage in the analysis it is a good practice to check the degree of correlation between the predictors in the model. The variance inflation factors (VIF) and the tolerance (1/VIF) are reported in Figure 31. Menard (1995) suggests that a tolerance of less than 0.20 is a cause for concern, and a tolerance of less than 0.10 almost certainly indicates a serious

```
      Source |       SS           df       MS          Number of obs   =     5,097
-------------+-------------------------------          F(14, 5082)     =    128.85
       Model |   325506963         14  23250497.3      Prob > F        =    0.0000
    Residual |   917001747      5,082  180441.115      R-squared       =    0.2620
-------------+-------------------------------          Adj R-squared   =    0.2599
       Total |  1242508710      5,096  243820.391      Root MSE        =    424.78

------------------------------------------------------------------------------
     zpaynu2 |      Coef.   Std. Err.      t    P>|t|     [95% Conf. Interval]
-------------+----------------------------------------------------------------
      zjbhrs |   9.559008   .8714275     10.97   0.000     7.850635    11.26738
      zjbcssm |  8.709623    .370681     23.50   0.000     7.982928    9.436317
      pacssm |   2.099019   .354503      5.92   0.000      1.40404    2.793998
    graduate |   195.6784  17.63807     11.09   0.000     161.1001    230.2566
     zregage |    6.51771   2.257654     2.89   0.004     2.091734    10.94368
             |
        wave |
          2  |   32.02204  26.09955      1.23   0.220    -19.14433     83.1884
          3  |   47.53042  26.53109      1.79   0.073    -4.481953     99.5428
          4  |   32.50858  27.03488      1.20   0.229    -20.49144     85.5086
          5  |   37.20393   27.6692      1.34   0.179    -17.03963    91.44749
          6  |   83.98088  28.31416      2.97   0.003     28.47293    139.4888
          7  |   72.86194  28.92154      2.52   0.012     16.16326    129.5606
          8  |    96.8642  29.82545      3.25   0.001     38.39346    155.3349
          9  |    139.523  31.31379      4.46   0.000     78.13451    200.9116
         10  |   138.2166    32.437      4.26   0.000     74.62611    201.8071
             |
       _cons |   135.0271  43.56656      3.10   0.002     49.61787    220.4363
------------------------------------------------------------------------------
```

Figure 30 Stata output: Pooled cross-sectional model: usual net pay (£) per month (adjusted for inflation) male full-time workers aged 25–35 waves 1–10

```
Variable |      VIF         1/VIF
-------------+-----------------------
    zjbhrs |     1.02      0.977645
   zjbcssm |     1.47      0.679207
    pacssm |     1.27      0.788431
  graduate |     1.39      0.720488
   zregage |     2.17      0.460210
      wave |
         2 |     1.69      0.590568
         3 |     1.72      0.583054
         4 |     1.78      0.561526
         5 |     1.87      0.534110
         6 |     2.00      0.500899
         7 |     2.15      0.464356
         8 |     2.35      0.426428
         9 |     2.47      0.405184
        10 |     2.70      0.370430
-------------+-----------------------
  Mean VIF |     1.86
```

Figure 31 Stata output: Variance inflation factors for the explanatory variables in the pooled cross-sectional model: usual net pay (£) per month (adjusted for inflation) male full-time workers aged 25–35 waves 1–10

collinearity problem.[4] The VIF values in the pooled cross-sectional model are well below the standard guidelines and the mean VIF is low. The VIF for the wave 10 dummy variable is not of concern as this is a control variable rather than an analytical variable.

Next we estimate the pooled cross-sectional model with robust standard errors. The beta values and their associated standard errors are reported in Figure 32. The coefficients of these two models are the same, but as is often the case when analysing panel data, the robust standard errors (see Figure 32 column 2) are larger than in the standard OLS model (see Figure 32 column 1). This is because the naïve OLS model calculates the standard errors as if there were 5,097 independent observations. In reality there are 825 men who are contributing to the data many times (i.e. up to 10 waves).

---

4 Similarly, Chatterjee and Hadi (2015) suggest that a VIF of over 10 should be of concern. More recently Paul Allison has suggested that he is concerned when VIF is above 2.50, see http://statisticalhorizons.com/multicollinearity (accessed 5 March 2017).

	(1)	(2)
	OLS b(se)	Clustered b(se)
zjbhrs	9.559***	9.559***
	(0.871)	(1.944)
zjbcssm	8.710***	8.710***
	(0.371)	(0.793)
pacssm	2.099***	2.099
	(0.355)	(1.116)
graduate	195.678***	195.678**
	(17.638)	(59.722)
zregage	6.518**	6.518
	(2.258)	(4.516)
1.wave	0.000	0.000
	(.)	(.)
2.wave	32.022	32.022*
	(26.100)	(13.903)
3.wave	47.530	47.530*
	(26.531)	(18.758)
4.wave	32.509	32.509
	(27.035)	(20.472)
5.wave	37.204	37.204
	(27.669)	(25.893)
6.wave	83.981**	83.981**
	(28.314)	(30.037)
7.wave	72.862*	72.862*
	(28.922)	(34.505)
8.wave	96.864**	96.864*
	(29.825)	(37.730)
9.wave	139.523***	139.523**
	(31.314)	(43.375)
10.wave	138.217***	138.217**
	(32.437)	(46.563)
_cons	135.027**	135.027
	(43.567)	(76.333)
n	5097	5097

Figure 32 Stata output: Pooled cross-sectional models of usual net pay (£) per month (adjusted for inflation) male full-time workers aged 25–35 waves 1–10 – summary of coefficients (b) and their standard errors (se)

In the next step of the analysis we prepare for estimating more comprehensive statistical models. We will begin to use the *xt* suite within Stata. The *xt* commands provide tools for analysing panel data. Historically, some research areas, such as certain branches of econometrics, called longitudinal data 'cross-sectional time series' data. In our experience this terminology usually leads to confusion. The term *x* stood for cross and *t* stood for time, and the abbreviation *xt* was used for cross-sectional time series following this terminology.

In order to use the *xt* suite in Stata it is convenient to declare the dataset to be panel data. the Stata command *xtset* is followed by the panel identifier (e.g. the respondent's identification number) and the time identifier. In the current example from the BHPS, the Stata command is *xtset pid wave*. Stata provides a report on the dataset and tells us that the panel is unbalanced (i.e. every man does not contribute 10 waves of data) and that some men have gaps in the run of their time variable.

It is always advisable to get a description of the panel before beginning to analyse the data, and the Stata *xtdes* command is especially useful. The output from the *xtdes* command is reported in Figure 33. There are 825 respondents (*n*) who make a maximum number of 10 contributions at different time points (*T*). The panel identifier is *pid* and Stata gives us a few examples of *pid*, the personal identification numbers. Stata gives some examples of the time variable *wave*. The 'Delta' or periodicity of the data is measured by the variable *wave* and the 'span' is 10 waves of observations. A useful part of the *xtdes* output is the relationship between the panel and the time variable. We see that the combination of *pid*wave* uniquely

```
    pid:  10024646, 10028005, ..., 1.071e+08              n =      825
   wave:  1, 2, ..., 10                                   T =       10
          Delta(wave)  = 1 unit
          Span(wave)   = 10 periods
          (pid*wave uniquely identifies each observation)

Distribution of T_i:   min     5%    25%      50%     75%     95%     max
                         1      1      3        7      10      10      10

    Freq.   Percent    Cum. |  Pattern
  ---------------------------+------------
     255     30.91    30.91 |  1111111111
      69      8.36    39.27 |  1.........
      27      3.27    42.55 |  .........1
      26      3.15    45.70 |  11........
      23      2.79    48.48 |  ......1111
      21      2.55    51.03 |  .......111
      18      2.18    53.21 |  111.......
      17      2.06    55.27 |  ........11
      16      1.94    57.21 |  ..11111111
     353     42.79   100.00 |  (other patterns)
  ---------------------------+------------
     825    100.00          |  XXXXXXXXXX
```

Figure 33 Stata output: *xtdes* male full-time workers aged 25–35 waves 1–10

identifies each observation and there are no duplicates. An alternative method of checking is to use Stata's *duplicates* or *isid* commands.

The distribution of the time variable is reported in the *xtdes* output. The minimum number of observations is 1 wave. The maximum number of observations is 10 waves. Fifty per cent of the sample contribute seven or fewer waves of data and over 25 per cent contribute a full ten waves of data.

We are already aware that this is an unbalanced panel. Specific patterns of observations are reported with *xtdes*. The most common 10 are reported in Figure 33, but Stata can report other patterns too. We can see that 255 of the 825 respondents (31 per cent) contributed 10 waves of data. By contrast 69 respondents were present in the first wave of the panel but did not contribute in any other waves, and 27 respondents were present only in the final wave of the panel.

The Stata command *xtsum* provides a summary of the panel data for the variable usual net pay per month. The results are reported in Figure 34. The first line of results are based on the 5,097 items of pooled data (i.e. every row of the data). The mean was £1059 with a standard deviation of £494. The minimum was £50 and the maximum was £9,742.

The second row of the output refers to the 825 respondents and is their 'between' information. This can be understood as the summary information that we would get if we collapsed the datasets and had one (summary) row with the mean values for each of the 825 respondents in the panel. The standard deviation of their individual means was £436. The lowest mean usual net pay per month for any of these 825 panel members was £223 and the maximum was £4,233.

The usual net pay per month within the panel varied between £ −753 and £7,374. This is not to say that any of these men earned negative wages. The within number is the deviation (i.e. the difference) between the individual's usual net pay per month in the particular wave of the panel and their mean (average) usual net pay per month across all of the waves they are in the panel ($x_{it} - \overline{x}_i$). Therefore, when the usual net pay per month in

```
Variable         |      Mean   Std. Dev.        Min        Max |    Observations
-----------------+--------------------------------------------------+----------------
zpaynu2  overall |  1058.978   493.7817   50.14124   9741.704 |   N   =       5097
         between |             435.5668   223.4477   4232.809 |   n   =        825
         within  |             241.674   -753.2659   7374.293 |   T-bar = 6.17818
```

Figure 34 Stata output: Summary of panel information (xtsum) for usual net pay (£) per month (adjusted for inflation) male full-time workers aged 25–35 waves 1–10

the current wave is lower than their mean across all waves of the panel, the within value will be negative. The *within* figures can be unintuitive because Stata calculates the within numbers as the deviation of each panel member's own mean plus the global mean ($x_{it} - \bar{x}_i + \bar{\bar{x}}$) to make them more readily comparable. The smaller within standard deviation indicates that the variation in the usual net pay per month variable is greater *between* these men than it is *within* them over time, as we might reasonably expect. Finally, *T-bar* is the mean number of contributions made to the panel (i.e. on average these men contributed six waves of data).

The between effects panel model can be estimated using the following Stata syntax:

xtreg zpaynu2 zjbhr zjbcssm pacssm graduate zregage i.wave, be

The between effects panel model is estimated on respondent averages or person averages. The results are reported in Figure 35. Stata reports that

```
Between regression (regression on group means)   Number of obs    =      5,097
Group variable: pid                              Number of groups =        825

R-sq:                                            Obs per group:
    within  = 0.0090                                          min =          1
    between = 0.3300                                          avg =        6.2
    overall = 0.1913                                          max =         10

                                                 F(14,810)        =      28.50
sd(u_i + avg(e_i.))=   359.5832                   Prob > F         =     0.0000

------------------------------------------------------------------------------
     zpaynu2 |      Coef.   Std. Err.      t    P>|t|     [95% Conf. Interval]
-------------+----------------------------------------------------------------
      zjbhrs |   14.09982   2.080738     6.78   0.000     10.01555    18.1841
      zjbcssm |  10.37977   .8820596    11.77   0.000     8.648383   12.11117
      pacssm |   .5965609   .7701049     0.77   0.439    -.9150758   2.108198
    graduate |   175.5115   40.03946     4.38   0.000     96.91819   254.1049
     zregage |   6.786292   4.743538     1.43   0.153    -2.524784   16.09737
             |
        wave |
          2  |  -161.7335   121.5139    -1.33   0.184    -400.2527    76.7857
          3  |  -25.15019   142.1006    -0.18   0.860     -304.079   253.7786
          4  |  -121.4847   162.0509    -0.75   0.454    -439.5738   196.6045
          5  |   364.7118   203.8055     1.79   0.074    -35.33747    764.761
          6  |   146.1435   198.3877     0.74   0.462    -243.2711   535.5581
          7  |  -90.28951   160.0381    -0.56   0.573    -404.4278   223.8488
          8  |  -118.0872    111.517    -1.06   0.290    -336.9835    100.8091
          9  |   108.0149   127.3982     0.85   0.397    -142.0546   358.0843
         10  |   3.870938   84.44292     0.05   0.963    -161.8818   169.6237
             |
       _cons |  -16.49739   104.6227    -0.16   0.875    -221.8609   188.8661
------------------------------------------------------------------------------
```

Figure 35 Stata output: Between effects model: usual net pay (£) per month (adjusted for inflation) male full-time workers aged 25–35 waves 1–10

the model is a 'regression on group means'. The 'groups' are the set of responses that the individual men made to the panel dataset. The model is estimated on the average information for each of the 825 men. The minimum number of waves that any man contributed was 1 and the maximum was 10. As we learnt from the output of *xtdes* and *xtsum* the average number of waves contributed was 6.2. The between effects model has a significant *F* statistic. The R^2 between measure (0.33) is the most relevant summary statistic. The regression table in the between effects model can be read in the same way as a standard cross-sectional regression model. The between effects model provides some information about the panel and plays a critical part in more comprehensive approaches to the analysis of panel data. Cameron and Trivedi (2010) note that the between effects models is infrequently reported in social science research.

In the next step of the analysis we estimate the fixed effects panel model. The model can be estimated with the following Stata syntax:

xtreg zpaynu2 zjbhr zjbcssm pacssm graduate zregage i.wave, fe

The output for the fixed effects panel model is reported in Figure 36. Stata provides a note that informs us that the explanatory variable *pacssm* (the male Cambridge Scale Score of the respondent's father's occupation when the respondent was aged 14) has been omitted from the model because of collinearity. The explanatory variable *pacssm* is time constant and therefore cannot be included in a fixed effects panel model.

The fixed effects panel model analyses variations within respondents. The model is estimated on 5,097 rows of data that have been contributed by the 825 men in the panel. The minimum number of waves that any man contributed was 1 and the maximum was 10. As we learnt from the output of *xtdes* and *xtsum*, and the between effects model, the average number of waves contributed was 6.2. There was a significant *F* test so we can reject the null hypothesis that the model coefficients are equal to zero. The individual errors, which Stata terms as *u_i*, are often correlated with the regressors, which Stata labels as *Xb*, in the fixed effects model output.

The output from *xtreg* provides three R^2 measures. These measures are based on the idea that R^2 summarizes the squared correlation between the actual and fitted values of the dependent variable, where the fitted values ignore the contribution of the individual-specific error (see Cameron and Trivedi, 2010). The first measure is the within R_w^2, the second

```
note: pacssm omitted because of collinearity

Fixed-effects (within) regression          Number of obs    =      5,097
Group variable: pid                         Number of groups =        825

R-sq:                                       Obs per group:
    within  = 0.0973                                    min =          1
    between = 0.0047                                    avg =        6.2
    overall = 0.0151                                    max =         10

                                            F(13,4259)       =      35.30
corr(u_i, Xb)  = -0.0716                    Prob > F         =     0.0000

------------------------------------------------------------------------------
    zpaynu2 |     Coef.   Std. Err.      t    P>|t|    [95% Conf. Interval]
------------+-----------------------------------------------------------------
     zjbhrs |  3.162216   .7598803     4.16   0.000     1.672455    4.651978
    zjbcssm |  .7083871   .4688331     1.51   0.131    -.2107702    1.627544
     pacssm |         0  (omitted)
   graduate | -68.42179   58.82074    -1.16   0.245    -183.7411    46.89752
    zregage |  9.779486   18.59062     0.53   0.599    -26.66781    46.22679
            |
       wave |
          2 |  33.77626   23.69473     1.43   0.154    -12.67775    80.23027
          3 |  50.54727   39.7453      1.27   0.204    -27.37422    128.4688
          4 |   36.4279   57.69603     0.63   0.528    -76.68639    149.5422
          5 |  38.07226   75.6673      0.50   0.615    -110.2751    186.4196
          6 |  85.96321   93.47347     0.92   0.358     -97.2935    269.2199
          7 |  87.99939   111.601      0.79   0.430    -130.7967    306.7955
          8 |  115.7779   130.037      0.89   0.373    -139.1623    370.7181
          9 |  161.5511   148.3231     1.09   0.276    -129.2394    452.3416
         10 |  172.5317   167.0504     1.03   0.302    -154.9742    500.0375
            |
      _cons |  751.7321   98.72638     7.61   0.000      558.177    945.2873
------------+-----------------------------------------------------------------
    sigma_u | 436.52027
    sigma_e | 251.17185
        rho | .75126958   (fraction of variance due to u_i)
------------------------------------------------------------------------------
F test that all u_i=0: F(824, 4259) = 12.59              Prob > F = 0.0000
```

Figure 36 Stata output: Fixed effects panel model: usual net pay (£) per month (adjusted for inflation) male full-time workers aged 25–35 waves 1–10

is the between R_b^2 and the third is the overall R_o^2. In the fixed effects model the within R_w^2 is maximized, the between R_b^2 is lower than in the between effects model and the overall R_w^2 is relatively low (see Figure 35 to compare the results with the between effects model). Cameron and Trivedi (2010) point out that the R_o^2 in a fixed effects panel model tends to be low because the calculation neglects the individual error. When the model above is estimated using the LSDV[5] approach, $R_o^2 = 0.78$.

---

5 This is easily achieved using Stata's *areg* command.

The regression table in the fixed effects model can be read as it would be in a standard output for a cross-sectional model. At the bottom of the table there is some extra information which is directly relevant to panel data analysis. The first measure *sigma_u* is the standard deviation of the residuals within groups, which in our case are the men in the panel. The second measure is *sigma_e*, which is the standard deviation of the residuals (or the overall error term) which Stata refers to as e_i.

The total variance of the error can be considered as $(sigma\_u)^2 + (sigma\_e)^2$. Therefore, the fraction of the variance of the error that is due to u_i is $(sigma\_u)^2 / ((sigma\_u)^2 + (sigma\_e)^2)$.

This can easily be calculated using Stata's *display* command:

display (436.52027^2)/((436.52027^2)+(251.17185^2))

Rho = 0.75, which is the proportion of the error variance that is due to u_i. Another way of thinking about this is that 75 per cent of the variance is at the panel level. We will return to rho when we discuss the random effects panel model. The final line of the output reports the results of an F test for the null hypothesis that all u_i = 0. The *p* value associated with the F test is significant and therefore we can reject the null hypothesis.

In the next step of the analysis we estimate the random effects panel model. The model can be estimated with the following Stata syntax[6]:

xtreg zpaynu2 zjbhr zjbcssm pacssm graduate zregage i.wave, re

The output for the random effects panel model is reported in Figure 37. The random effects panel model is estimated on 5,097 rows of data that have been contributed by the 825 men in the panel. Once again the

---

6 This specification invokes Stata's default estimation settings for the *xtreg* command, which uses an algorithm known as 'generalized least squares'. A number of different estimation strategies can be used to fit random effects models, including many that are available through alternative specifications in Stata. In social science applications, different settings will typically lead to slight, but not usually substantial, differences in estimated model parameters. For extended discussion see Hox, Moerbeek and Van De Schoot (2010).

```
Random-effects GLS regression              Number of obs     =      5,097
Group variable: pid                        Number of groups  =        825

R-sq:                                      Obs per group:
     within  = 0.0875                                    min =          1
     between = 0.2458                                    avg =        6.2
     overall = 0.2291                                    max =         10

                                           Wald chi2(14)     =     688.95
corr(u_i, X)  = 0 (assumed)                Prob > chi2       =     0.0000

------------------------------------------------------------------------------
     zpaynu2 |    Coef.    Std. Err.     z    P>|z|    [95% Conf. Interval]
-------------+----------------------------------------------------------------
      zjbhrs |  4.095316   .7257752    5.64   0.000    2.672823    5.51781
     zjbcssm |  3.190851   .4147334    7.69   0.000    2.377988   4.003713
      pacssm |  3.949381   .7204518    5.48   0.000    2.537321    5.36144
    graduate |  202.0455   30.88336    6.54   0.000    141.5152   262.5758
     zregage |  9.659352    4.59312    2.10   0.035    .6570023    18.6617
             |
        wave |
           2 |  32.94832   16.59421    1.99   0.047    .4242625   65.47238
           3 |  48.03321   18.53548    2.59   0.010    11.70434   84.36207
           4 |  31.86777   21.25793    1.50   0.134   -9.797011   73.53255
           5 |  31.99669   24.47987    1.31   0.191   -15.98297   79.97635
           6 |  78.77641   27.94861    2.82   0.005    23.99814   133.5547
           7 |  77.89485   31.66425    2.46   0.014    15.83407   139.9556
           8 |  100.9134   35.62999    2.83   0.005    31.07988   170.7469
           9 |   144.7248     39.838    3.63   0.000    66.64376   222.8058
          10 |  153.3713    44.0223    3.48   0.000    67.08919   239.6534
             |
        _cons |  441.8567   45.78108    9.65   0.000    352.1274   531.5859
-------------+----------------------------------------------------------------
     sigma_u |  331.89925
     sigma_e |  251.17185
         rho |  .63584801   (fraction of variance due to u_i)
------------------------------------------------------------------------------
```

Figure 37 Stata output: Random effects panel model: usual net pay (£) per month (adjusted for inflation) male full-time workers aged 25–35 waves 1–10

minimum number of waves that any man contributed was 1 and the maximum was 10, and 6.2 was the average number of waves contributed. The chi-square test reported in the output for the random effects panel model is analogous to the F test in the fixed effects panel model. The chi-square value can be rescaled to F by dividing it by the number of degrees of freedom. There was a significant chi-square test so we can reject the null hypothesis that the model coefficients are equal to zero.

Stata reminds us that an assumption of the random effects panel model is that there is a zero correlation between the unobserved effects and the observed effects, and states '$corr(u\_i, X) = 0$ *(assumed)*' in the output.

In the random effects panel model, the within R_w^2 is slightly lower than in the fixed effects panel model (see Figure 36). The between R_b^2 in the random effects panel model is larger than in the fixed effects panel model and closer to the R_b^2 in the between effects model (see Figure 36 and Figure 35). More of the overall variance is explained in the random effects panel model (R_o^2). The regression table can be read in the usual way. The Cambridge Scale Score (male) of the respondent's father's occupation when the respondent was aged 14 is now estimated because time-constant variables can be included in random effects panel models.

The final part of the output includes some extra information which is directly relevant to panel data analysis. The total error variance can be considered as $(sigma\_u)^2 + (sigma\_e)^2$, and therefore, the fraction of the variance that is due to u_i is $(sigma\_u)^2 / ((sigma\_u)^2 + (sigma\_e)^2)$.

This can easily be calculated using Stata's *display* command

display $(331.89925\char94 2)/((331.89925\char94 2)+(251.17185\char94 2))$

Rho = 0.64, which is the fraction of the variance that is due to u_i. Another way of thinking about this is that 64 per cent of the error variance is at the panel level. Rho is analogous to an intra-class correlation, or ICC, as it is known in other areas such as the literature on multilevel modelling (see Goldstein, Browne and Rasbash, 2002). In practice rho will change depending on how well the explanatory variables capture the between and within influences on the outcome. When the model includes explanatory variables that mainly reflect the characteristics of the panel respondents, the value of rho may be smaller. When the model includes explanatory variables that mainly reflect things that change over time, rho may tend to be larger.

When rho is zero the panel-level variance component is unimportant and the panel estimator is not different from the pooled (i.e. cross-sectional) estimator. In our experience it is almost never the case that rho is zero when estimating a model using a genuine panel dataset. One notable exception is reported in Exeter (2004), where the units in the panel were geographical areas. Unexpectedly there was no evidence of clustering over time, which was probably due to the large gaps between the time points in the data.

Having estimated the random effects panel model, we can now undertake the Lagrange multiplier test for random effects (see Breusch and Pagan, 1980). The Lagrange multiplier test is a formal test that the variance Var(u) = 0. The Stata command is *xttest0*, and the results of this test are reported in Figure 38. The estimated variance u is 110157.1

```
Breusch and Pagan Lagrangian multiplier test for random effects

    zpaynu2[pid,t] = Xb + u[pid] + e[pid,t]

Estimated results:
                  |        Var       sd = sqrt(Var)
         ---------+-----------------------------
          zpaynu2 |     243820.4         493.7817
                e |      63087.3         251.1718
                u |     110157.1         331.8993

    Test:    Var(u) = 0
                          chibar2(01) =    6525.74
                      Prob > chibar2 =     0.0000
```

Figure 38 Stata output: Breusch and Pagan Lagrangian multiplier test random effects panel model: usual net pay (£) per month (adjusted for inflation) male full-time workers aged 25–35 waves 1–10

(which is *sigma_u²*). The chi-square test is significant so we can reject the null hypothesis that variance Var(u) = 0. Given that we are modelling individual-level repeated contacts data, it is not at all surprising that there is a large amount of panel-level variance.

In the final part of this analysis we step back and consider the results of the range of models of usual net pay per month for this panel of male full-time workers. The OLS model is a pooled analysis of the panel data. The between effects model focuses on differences between the men in the panel. The fixed effects panel model focuses on *within-person* effects, and the random effects panel model draws on both *between* and *within* information. Figure 39 reports the coefficients estimated by each of the models. The number of hours normally worked per week, *zjbhrs*, is significant in all of the models. It is more important in the between effects model where the emphasis is *between* respondents. By contrast it is less important in the fixed effects panel model where the emphasis is on changes *within* respondents. It is worth noting that the importance of *zjbhrs* increases in the random effects panel model, which draws on both between-respondents information and within-respondents information.

The Cambridge Scale Score (males) for the respondent's present job is significant in the OLS model and the between effects model. It is not significant in the fixed effects panel model, where the emphasis of the analysis is on *within-person* change. The Cambridge Scale Score (males) for the respondent's present job is significant in the random effects panel model, which draws on *between-respondent* information.

	OLS b(se)	BE b(se)	FE b(se)	RE b(se)
zjbhrs	9.559***	14.100***	3.162***	4.095***
	(0.871)	(2.081)	(0.760)	(0.726)
zjbcssm	8.710***	10.380***	0.708	3.191***
	(0.371)	(0.882)	(0.469)	(0.415)
pacssm	2.099***	0.597	0.000	3.949***
	(0.355)	(0.770)	(.)	(0.720)
graduate	195.678***	175.512***	−68.422	202.046***
	(17.638)	(40.039)	(58.821)	(30.883)
zregage	6.518**	6.786	9.779	9.659*
	(2.258)	(4.744)	(18.591)	(4.593)
1.wave	0.000	0.000	0.000	0.000
	(.)	(.)	(.)	(.)
2.wave	32.022	−161.733	33.776	32.948*
	(26.100)	(121.514)	(23.695)	(16.594)
3.wave	47.530	−25.150	50.547	48.033**
	(26.531)	(142.101)	(39.745)	(18.535)
4.wave	32.509	−121.485	36.428	31.868
	(27.035)	(162.051)	(57.696)	(21.258)
5.wave	37.204	364.712	38.072	31.997
	(27.669)	(203.806)	(75.667)	(24.480)
6.wave	83.981**	146.143	85.963	78.776**
	(28.314)	(198.388)	(93.473)	(27.949)
7.wave	72.862*	−90.290	87.999	77.895*
	(28.922)	(160.038)	(111.601)	(31.664)
8.wave	96.864**	−118.087	115.778	100.913**
	(29.825)	(111.517)	(130.037)	(35.630)
9.wave	139.523***	108.015	161.551	144.725***
	(31.314)	(127.398)	(148.323)	(39.838)
10.wave	138.217***	3.871	172.532	153.371***
	(32.437)	(84.443)	(167.050)	(44.022)
_cons	135.027**	−16.497	751.732***	441.857***
	(43.567)	(104.623)	(98.726)	(45.781)
n	5097	5097	5097	5097

OLS: Pooled Regression Model
BE: Between Effects Model
FE: Fixed Effects Panel Model
RE: Random Effects Panel Model

Figure 39 Stata output: Coefficients (b) and their standard errors (se) from the pooled regression model, the between effects model, the fixed effects panel model and the random effects panel model – usual net pay (£) per month (adjusted for inflation) male full-time workers aged 25–35

The Cambridge Scale Score (male) of the respondent's father's occupation when the respondent was aged 14, *pacssm*, is fixed in time and cannot be estimated in a fixed effects panel model. Being a graduate is significant in the between effects model. It is not significant in the fixed effects panel model, which emphasizes *within-person* change. It is worth noting that there were 97 graduates in wave 1 and 109 graduates in wave 10. Some of the men became graduates during the panel. In the analysis of panel data it is always worth considering variables which change little in time, and to think about the role that these variables might play in an analysis. On closer inspection we found that only 11 men changed their educational level. We might expect that this change was from non-graduate to graduate, but in two cases the respondent changed from being a graduate to a non-graduate. This underlines the requirement for the quantitative longitudinal data analyst to know their data and to undertake suitable detective work when it is required. Researchers should clearly document how they make appropriate alterations to anomalies in research data.

In our experience there are variables in social science analyses that are not fixed in time but change little during the panel and being a graduate is one example. As these variables change for some individuals they can be included in the fixed effects panel model. The estimation procedure is identifying on a small number of 'switchers' in the panel however, and we would be cautious about these results.

Comparing fixed effects panel models and random effects panel models

Having introduced some approaches to analysing panel data we now turn our attention to the frequently asked question 'Which model should be used?' Gelman and Hill (2007), two leading statisticians, comment that the statistical literature is full of confusing and contradictory advice. Searle, Casella and McCulloch (1992) assert that because of conflicting definitions, it is no surprise that clear answers to the question 'fixed or random effects?' are unusual. In this section we touch upon some of the pertinent issues and offer some practicable advice for analysing quantitative longitudinal data.

Researchers routinely ask, 'Should I choose a fixed effects panel model or a random effects panel model?' The answer depends on what the data analyst is attempting to model. The fixed effects panel model focuses upon the within-subject change, whereas the random effects panel model is influenced by both within- and between-subject patterns, and both have potential advantages and limitations (Clark and Linzer, 2015). In some cases choosing between them will be informed by the researcher's theoretical understanding of the social process that is being analysed, but sometimes there will not be an obvious or clear theoretically informed view of which estimator should be preferred, and there might not be a straightforward means of evaluating alternative approaches.

Following the guidance from the argument in mainstream econometrics about the key technical differences between the fixed effects panel model and the random effects panel model, a common procedure within economics is to use the Hausman test to adjudicate between these panel models (see Wooldridge, 2010; Hausman, 1978). Greene (2012b) states that the Hausman test is a useful device for determining the preferred specification of a common effects model, and it is implemented in Stata and some other software packages. The theoretical idea that informs this approach is that the test compares an estimator that is known to be consistent (β_{fe}), with another estimator (β_{re}) that is efficient under the assumption being tested. The conventional theory in econometrics proposes a null hypothesis that the estimator β_{re} is an efficient and consistent estimate of the true parameters. If this is the case, there will be no systematic differences between the two estimators β_{fe} and β_{re}. If systematic differences in the estimates exist, then there is reason to doubt the assumption that there is no correlation between the observed variables and the unobserved effects (Baum, 2006).

The following Stata syntax illustrates how the Hausman test can be performed after estimating a fixed effects panel model and storing the estimates, and then estimating a random effects panel model and storing the estimates:

```
xtreg y x1 x2, fe
estimates store fixed_effects
xtreg y x1 x2, re
estimates store random_effects
hausman fixed_effects random_effects
```

Drawing on a subset of data from Cornwell and Rupert (1988) we estimate two simple panel data models. The first is a fixed effects panel model and the second is the random effects panel model. The outcome variable is log wages and the models include three explanatory variables, full-time work experience in years, the number of weeks worked in the year and a dummy variable indicating whether the respondent is in a 'blue-collar' occupation. The results of the two models are reported in Table 3.

Table 3 Coefficients (β) and their standard errors (se) from the fixed effects panel model and the random effects panel model – log wages

	(1) Fixed effects β_{fe} (s.e.)	(2) Random effects β_{re} (s.e.)
Ft work experience (years)	0.097	0.057
	(0.001)	(0.001)
Weeks worked	0.001	0.002
	(0.001)	(0.001)
Blue-collar occupation	-0.021	-0.108
	(0.014)	(0.016)
Constant	4.709	5.523
	(0.038)	(0.047)
n	4165	4165

Data from Cornwell and Rupert (1988).

Table 4 Hausman test comparing estimates for the fixed effects panel model with the random effects panel model – log wages

	(1) Fixed effects β_{fe}	(2) Random effects β_{re}	(3) Difference $\beta_{fe} - \beta_{re}$	(4) S.E. Difference $\beta_{fe} - \beta_{re}$
Ft work experience (years)	0.097	0.057	0.040	0.001
Weeks worked	0.001	0.002	−0.001	0.000
Blue-collar occupation	−0.021	−0.108	0.087	0.007
$\chi^2 = 1609.7$ at 3 d.f.				
$p < 0.001$				

Data from Cornwell and Rupert (1988).

The two panel models contain common effects and the comparisons are reported in Table 4.

The Hausman test reports a chi-square of 1609.7 at 3 d.f., which is highly significant ($p < 0.001$). Therefore, in this example we can reject the null hypothesis $H_0: \beta_{fe} = \beta_{re}$, and for this analysis the conventional theory would favour the fixed effect panel model (see Wooldridge, 2010).

Greene (1999) illustrates the use of the Hausman test to compare two models analysing costs in the airline industry. The data are a panel of six airlines with 15 time points. The outcome measure is the log total cost (per $1000). The results are presented in Table 5. There are very small differences in the beta values in each of the two models. In a simple sense this indicates that the models are very similar. In this example the chi-square value is not significant and therefore we cannot reject the null hypothesis H_o: $\beta_{fe} = \beta_{re}$. For this analysis the test statistic provides reasonable grounds to favour the random effects panel model. Expressed theoretically, in this example β_{fe} is known to be consistent, but β_{re} is both a consistent and an efficient estimate of the true parameters.

The situation is usually less clear in genuine panel data analyses. In practice, there is usually a trade-off when choosing between using fixed effects panel models and random effects panel models. A consistent estimator has the statistical property that as the number of data points increases it converges on the true value. A statistically efficient estimate has the smallest asymptotic variance. In theory, the fixed effects estimator is consistent but less efficient than the random effects estimator. The random effects estimator is efficient but might not be consistent. Therefore, there might be a trade-off between choosing an estimate that is consistent but not efficient, rather than an estimate that is not consistent but efficient. Cameron and Trivedi (2005) remark that historically there have been differences within academic disciplines and that fixed effects models have usually been preferred in economics.

There are a number of technical commentaries that cast doubt over the suitability of the conventional use of the Hausman test, for adjudicating between fixed and random effects models. Fielding (2004) concluded that the widely held belief that a significant Hausman test implies that a random effects framework be abandoned is somewhat premature. Clarke et al. (2010) concluded that additional aspects of model misspecification make a significant Hausman test result hard to meaningfully interpret, and therefore, it becomes difficult to reliably choose between estimation approaches. This point is echoed by Skrondal and Rabe-Hesketh (2004). In our experience we have observed few examples such as in Table 5, where the Hausman test is not significant. This is because the Hausman approach tests whether the correlation between the observed variables and the unobserved effect equals zero. Angrist and Pischke (2009) remind us there will ordinarily be some small level of correlation between the observed variables and the unobserved effects.

A key theoretical question is whether the researcher is aiming for an analysis that is largely based upon a summary of the within-subject change.

Table 5 Hausman test comparing a fixed effects panel model with a random effects panel model – log total cost (per $1000)

	(1) Fixed effects β_{fe}	(2) Random effects β_{re}	(3) Difference $\beta_{fe} - \beta_{re}$	(4) S.E. Difference $\beta_{fe} - \beta_{re}$
Log output revenue index (passenger miles)	0.919	0.907	0.013	0.015
Log price of fuel	0.417	0.423	−0.005	0.006
Load factor (average capacity of the fleet)	−1.070	−1.064	−0.006	0.026
$\chi^2 = 3.24$ at 3 d.f.				
p = 0.356				

Data from Greene (1999).

The conventional approach in economics prioritizes the within-subject change, but there could be scenarios where model parameters that capture a balance of between and within effects are more useful. Statisticians outside of economics have made arguments against the conventional position. Gelman and Hill (2007) strongly advocate random effects models. Clarke et al. (2010) conclude that while the fixed effects approach has advantages, it limits the type of research questions that can be addressed. They state that where rich data are available, random effects models have qualities that are close to fixed effects models and facilitate the investigation of a wider range of research questions. In more recent methodological work, Clark and Linzer (2015) state that the most common objection to the use of random effects is the violation of the technical assumption that observed variables are uncorrelated with unobserved effects. They conclude that this is an insufficient justification to prefer a fixed effects model over a random effects model. This is because their simulations show that even in the presence of rather extreme violations of this assumption, the random effects model performs no worse than the fixed effects model.

Recently there has been renewed attention in what is sometimes referred to as the Mundlak or the Mundlak-Chamberlain approach (see Mundlak, 1978; Chamberlain, 1979). We will use the term 'Mundlak approach'. In essence the Mundlak approach helps to satisfy the assumption in the random effects panel model that the observed effects are uncorrelated with the unobserved effects. This is achieved through the inclusion of the means of the respondent's time-varying variables within the random effects panel model. More technical accounts are available in Wooldridge (2005, 2010).

A shortcut Stata module for the Mundlak approach is available through the RePEC IDEAS website.[7] The module estimates random effects models adding group means of independent variables to the model. Returning to the example from Cornwell and Rupert (1988), a comparison of the coefficients and standard errors of the fixed effects panel model and the random effects panel model (both with and without the Mundlak adjustment) are presented in Table 6. The random effects panel model with the Mundlak

Table 6 Coefficients (β) and their standard errors (se) from the fixed effects panel model, the random effects panel model with Mundlak adjustment, and the random effects panel model – log wages

	(1) Fixed effects β_{fe} (s.e.)		(2) Random effects with Mundlak β_{mre} (s.e.)		(3) Random effects β_{re} (s.e.)	
Ft work Experience (years)	0.097 (0.001)	***	0.097 (0.001)	***	0.057 (0.001)	***
Weeks worked	0.001 (0.001)	*	0.001 (0.001)	*	0.002 (0.001)	**
Blue-collar occupation	−0.021 (0.014)		−0.021 (0.014)		−0.108 (0.016)	***
Individual's mean ft work experience (years)			−0.090 (0.002)	***		
Individual's mean weeks worked			0.010 (0.004)	**		
Individual's mean blue-collar occupation			−0.316 (0.034)	***		
Constant	4.709 (0.038)	***	6.164 (0.212)	***	5.523 (0.047)	***
n	4165		4165		4165	

Data from Cornwell and Rupert (1988).

---

7 See http://fmwww.bc.edu/repec/bocode/m/mundlak.ado (accessed 19 May 2016).

adjustment will recover the same coefficients and standard errors as the fixed effects panel model. This is appealing because it responds to the concerns raised by the Hausman test result (reported in Table 4) while retaining the other attractive features of the random effects model (such as the capacity to include fixed-in-time explanatory variables). In the Mundlak formulation, we see that each of the three variables measuring individual respondent's means is significant. If we carry out a global test that these variables are equal to zero, we get a highly significant chi-square value of 2623.45 at 3 degrees of freedom. In a recent blog post Enrique Pinzon, a senior econometrician at StataCorp, suggested that this method of testing provides an alternative to the Hausman test.[8]

Returning briefly to the example from Greene (1999) a comparison of the coefficients and standard errors of the fixed effects panel model and the random effects panel model (both with and without the Mundlak adjustment) are presented in Table 7. We can see that the three group mean variables, which in this example are the individual means for each of the six airlines, are not significant in the random effects model with the Mundlak adjustment. Furthermore, a global test of the means similarly reveals that they are not significant with a chi-square value of 3.25 at 3 degrees of freedom (p = 0.36).

A further attraction of the Mundlak approach is illustrated in Table 8. In the random effects panel model with the Mundlak adjustment the 'consistent' estimates from the fixed effects panel model are recovered for the effects of full-time work experience (years), weeks worked and being in a blue-collar occupation; however, it is also possible to estimate the effects of being female, which is time constant in this dataset.

An alternative to the Mundlak approach was proposed by Allison (2009), which is sometimes referred to as the 'hybrid transformation' or 'hybrid model'. In essence it transforms the original independent variables into group mean deviations in addition to including the group means as additional explanatory variables. The hybrid model can be estimated using the *mundlak* command in Stata with the option *hybrid*.

While the Mundlak correction fits all group means, it is also possible to fit only some group means, for example as a response to model fitting evaluations. Recently, Bell and Jones (2015) have come out as strong

---

8 See http://blog.stata.com/2015/10/29/fixed-effects-or-random-effects-the-mundlak-approach/ (accessed 19 May 2016).

Table 7 Coefficients (β) and their standard errors (se) from the fixed effects panel model, the random effects panel model with Mundlak adjustment, and the random effects panel model – log total cost (per $1000)

	(1) Fixed effects β_{fe} (s.e.)		(2) Random effects with Mundlak β_{mre} (s.e.)		(3) Random effects β_{re} (s.e.)	
Log output revenue	0.919	***	0.919	***	0.907	***
index (passenger miles)	(0.030)		(0.030)		(0.026)	
Log price of fuel	0.417	***	0.417	***	0.423	***
	(0.015)		(0.015)		(0.014)	
Load factor (average	−1.070	***	−1.070	***	−1.064	***
capacity of the fleet)	(0.202)		(0.202)		(0.200)	
Airline mean log			−0.137			
output revenue index			(0.113)			
(passenger miles)						
Airline mean			−5.941			
log price of fuel			(4.479)			
Airline mean			−0.681			
Load factor (average			(2.751)			
capacity of the fleet)						
Constant	9.714	***	85.808		9.628	***
	(0.230)		(56.482)		(0.210)	
n	90		90		90	

Data from Greene (1999).

advocates of random effects models, which include bespoke group mean adjustments for the correlation between observed and unobserved effects. They take the strong view that there are few, if any, occasions in which the fixed effects model is preferable to the random effects model. They further state that if the assumptions required for the random effects model are met, it is preferable due to its greater flexibility.

At a practical level the lack of a clear prescription from the statistical literature can be immobilizing for social scientists engaged in applied quantitative longitudinal data analysis. We therefore offer the following advice. Proceed by thinking about your research question and the scope and limitations of the available data. Where possible your choice between the fixed effects panel model and the random effects panel model should

Table 8 Coefficients (β) and their standard errors (se) from the fixed effects panel model, the random effects panel model with Mundlak adjustment, and the random effects panel model – log wages (including a time-constant explanatory variable – female)

	(1) Fixed effects β_{fe} (s.e.)		(2) Random effects with Mundlak β_{mre} (s.e.)		(3) Random effects β_{re} (s.e.)	
Ft work	0.097	***	0.097	***	0.052	***
experience (years)	(0.001)		(0.001)		(0.001)	
Weeks worked	0.001	*	0.001	*	0.002	**
	(0.001)		(0.001)		(0.001)	
Blue-collar	−0.021		−0.021		−0.124	***
Occupation	(0.014)		(0.014)		(0.016)	
Female	0.000		−0.498	***	−0.323	***
	(.)		(0.042)		(0.055)	
Individual's mean ft			−0.091	***		
work experience (years)			(0.002)			
Individual's mean			0.004			
weeks worked			(0.004)			
Individual's mean			−0.344	***		
blue-collar occupation			(0.031)			
Constant	4.709	***	6.569	***	5.671	***
	(0.038)		(0.194)		(0.048)	
n	4165		4165		4165	

be informed by your theoretical understanding of the social process that is being analysed. Estimate a series of theoretically plausible statistical models and carefully compare their results. The econometrician Steve Pudney suggests that data analysts should carefully examine the differences between β_{fe} and β_{re}, and if they are suitably small, then the random effects model should be chosen even if the Hausman test is significant. In these situations plotting the two sets of estimates might also be helpful. Our advice when comparing the specification of the two common effects models is that the quantitative longitudinal data analyst should report both sets of estimates and undertake the Hausman test but not be strictly bound by it. It is also sensible to consider extension to the random effects model such as the Mundlak approach. A clear statement should be made justifying the choice of model and the results should be made available within the auxiliary information on the data analytical process, for example in an appendix posted in a repository.

Nevertheless, in some situations it will not be possible to follow this advice. For example, when undertaking analyses with a binary outcome, the results of the fixed effects panel model and the random effects panel model may not be a common comparison (we will return to this issue in the next section). Some models, for example the random effects ordered logit model, do not have a fixed effects counterpart. In these situations the quantitative longitudinal data analyst should report clear justifications for their choice of model.

Panel models for binary outcomes

In this section we turn our attention to analysing panel data with binary outcomes (i.e. 0,1). We stated earlier in this chapter that a panel regression model is an extension of the simpler cross-sectional regression model. A panel logistic regression model is an extension of the standard logistic (or logit) model that is used to analyse cross-sectional data with a binary outcome variable.

We will now illustrate a panel logistic regression model using a small teaching panel dataset, the Women's Employment Dataset.[9] The data mirror a real example of panel data analysis reported in Davies et al. (1992). The dataset is a panel of 155 married women, who were observed for up to 14 annual waves (1,580 rows of data). Forty-six per cent of the women contributed in all 14 waves. The mean age of the women was 33 in the first wave, the panel began in 1975, and one wave of data was collected each year. Descriptive statistics are provided in Figure 40. The data are declared as a panel and set for subsequent analysis using the Stata command:

   xtset case time

The Stata output for a pooled cross-sectional logistic regression model of wife's employment (*femp==1* is employed) is reported in Figure 41. The

---

9 The dataset wemp.dta is available at http://www.restore.ac.uk/Longitudinal/data/wemp_s2.dat (accessed 1 June 2016).

```
Variable   Obs  Unique   Mean    Min  Max  Label
----------------------------------------------------------------------
case      1580    155  517.7411    1 1003  id
femp      1580      2  .6455696    0    1  wife employment
mune      1580      2  .0740506    0    1  husband unemployed
time      1580     14     7.2      0   13  year of observation-1975
und1      1580      2  .0746835    0    1  woman has a child aged under 1 year
und5      1580      2  .2974684    0    1  woman has a child aged under 5 years
age       1580     43  36.01013   18   60  woman's age
regage    1580     43  18.01013    0   42  woman's age - 18
----------------------------------------------------------------------
```

Figure 40 Stata output: Compact codebook for the women's employment dataset

```
Logistic regression                          Number of obs   =      1,580
                                             LR chi2(3)      =     297.67
                                             Prob > chi2     =     0.0000
Log likelihood = -878.39352                  Pseudo R2       =     0.1449

----------------------------------------------------------------------
     femp |    Coef.   Std. Err.      z    P>|z|    [95% Conf. Interval]
----------+-----------------------------------------------------------
   1.mune | -1.706271  .2357956    -7.24   0.000   -2.168422   -1.24412
   1.und5 | -1.784628  .1401293   -12.74   0.000   -2.059276   -1.50998
   regage | -.0055946  .0073955    -0.76   0.449   -.0200896   .0089005
    _cons |  1.423699  .1723462     8.26   0.000    1.085907   1.761491
----------------------------------------------------------------------
```

Figure 41 Stata output: Pooled logistic regression model wife employed

model includes 1,580 rows of data which are assumed to be independent observations. The likelihood ratio chi-square (LR chi^2) is 297.67. This measure can be considered to be analogous to the F test in a standard linear regression model. The deviance of the current model is $-2 *$ log likelihood$_{model}$ (i.e. $-2 * -878.39 = 1756.79$). The deviance of the null model (i.e. the model with only the constant) is $-2 *$ log likelihood$_{null}$ (i.e. $-2 * -1027.23 = 2054.46$). The log likelihood$_{null}$ is not displayed in the standard Stata output but it can be recovered as it is stored as a scalar and can be displayed using the Stata command:

display e(ll_0)

The LR chi^2 value is the Deviance$_{null}$ − Deviance$_{model}$ (i.e. 2054.46−1756.79 = 297.67). There are 3 degrees of freedom because there are three explanatory variables in the model. The LR chi^2 value is significant and indicates that all of the model coefficients are unequal to zero (in the same way as we would interpret a significant F test in a standard linear regression model).

The McFadden's pseudo R^2 is reported for logistic regression models (see McFadden, 1973). Logistic regression models are not estimated using OLS, and therefore, the R^2 measures that are calculated are not the same as R^2 in a standard linear regression model. The prefix 'pseudo' is appended to the title of the measures because pseudo R^2 measures behave like a conventional R^2, and higher values indicate that the model has explained more of the variability in the outcome variable. Most pseudo R^2 measures do not cover the full range of values from 0 to 1. There are several pseudo R^2 measures, and Smithson (2003) pithily remarks that there has been something of a cottage industry in model fit statistics for logistic regression. Long and Freese (2014) provide an excellent overview of the scope and limitations of these measures. Stata reports McFadden's measure by default but a range of pseudo R^2 measures which can be accessed using the *fitstat* command.[10]

Figure 42 reports the marginal effects (adjusted predictions) for the pooled logistic regression model of wife's employment. There is a dramatic negative effect of having an unemployed husband (*mune==1*), which

```
Adjusted predictions                          Number of obs   =      1,580
Model VCE      : OIM

Expression   : Pr(femp), predict()
at           : 0.mune          =     .9259494 (mean)
               1.mune          =     .0740506 (mean)
               0.und5          =     .7025316 (mean)
               1.und5          =     .2974684 (mean)
               regage          =     18.01013 (mean)

------------------------------------------------------------------------------
             |            Delta-method
             |    Margin   Std. Err.      z    P>|z|     [95% Conf. Interval]
-------------+----------------------------------------------------------------
        mune |
          0  |   .6882756   .0130518    52.73   0.000     .6626945    .7138567
          1  |   .2861409   .0465328     6.15   0.000     .1949382    .3773436
             |
        und5 |
          0  |   .7679176   .0135043    56.86   0.000     .7414496    .7943855
          1  |   .3570851   .0249988    14.28   0.000     .3080884    .4060818
------------------------------------------------------------------------------
```

Figure 42 Stata output: Margins (adjusted predictions at means) for the pooled logistic regression model wife employed

---

10 The package *fitstat* can be installed using the following Stata syntax *net install spost13_ado.pkg*

reduced the woman's predicted probability of employment from 0.69 to 0.29. Similarly, having a child under age five reduces a wife's probability of employment from 0.77 to 0.36.

The next step in the analysis is to estimate the pooled logistic regression model with robust standard errors. The Stata syntax is:

logit femp i.mune i.und5 regage, cluster(case)

A cursory examination of the results reported in Figure 43 illustrates that the robust standard errors for the coefficients in the pooled logistic regression model are larger than in Figure 41. The output recognizes that there are 155 women contributing 1,580 rows of data. In this output, Stata reports a 'log pseudolikelihood' instead of the usual 'log likelihood'. The log pseudolikelihood is the same as the log likelihood in Figure 41. In other analyses of clustered data the likelihood may behave differently, and therefore, it is referred to as a 'pseudolikelihood' (a mathematical explication is provided in Skinner, Holt and Smith, 1989).

A random effects logistic regression panel model can be estimated in Stata with the following syntax:

xtlogit femp i.mune i.und5 regage, re noskip

The results of the model are reported in Figure 44. There are 1,580 rows of data, which have been contributed by 155 wives. The minimum number of waves was 1, the maximum was 14 and the average was 10. The output

```
Logistic regression                        Number of obs    =      1,580
                                           Wald chi2(3)     =      78.88
                                           Prob > chi2      =     0.0000
Log pseudolikelihood = -878.39352          Pseudo R2        =     0.1449

                           (Std. Err. adjusted for 155 clusters in case)
-----------------------------------------------------------------------------
             |               Robust
        femp |      Coef.   Std. Err.      z    P>|z|     [95% Conf. Interval]
-------------+---------------------------------------------------------------
      1.mune |  -1.706271   .4100495    -4.16   0.000    -2.509953   -.9025888
      1.und5 |  -1.784628   .2285538    -7.81   0.000    -2.232585   -1.336671
      regage |  -.0055946   .0155999    -0.36   0.720    -.0361699    .0249807
       _cons |   1.423699    .310223     4.59   0.000     .8156731    2.031725
-----------------------------------------------------------------------------
```

Figure 43 Stata output: Pooled logistic regression model wife employed with robust standard errors

reports that this is a random effects logistic regression and that the grouping variable was *case*. The random effect was assumed to have been drawn from the Gaussian distribution and the model was estimated using *mvaghermite* as an integration method. This is a standard approach but Stata also supports some other estimation methods.

The random effects logit panel model is calculated using quadrature. Quadrature is an approximation whose accuracy depends partially on the number of 'integration points' that are used. In this example the standard 12 points are used (*i.e. Integration pts.* = 12). In Stata it is possible to compare a range of models using different numbers of integration points. A convenient way is to use the Stata command *quadchk*, which checks the sensitivity of quadrature approximation. It is worth being cautious if the estimates of a model differ substantially when a different number of integration points are used to estimate a model (a clear passage on this issue is presented in Barry, Francis and Davies, 1989). In analyses there may often be small differences in estimates between models. In this example there are miniscule differences of 0.0009 in the estimate of *mune* and 0.0003 in the estimate of *und5*, between the model with 12 points of integration and the model with 16 points of integration.

An overall LR test is calculated for the model. We have used the Stata *xtlogit* option *noskip* to get an LR chi2 test rather than the default Wald chi-square test as this will help us to understand some other parts of the model output. The LR chi2 test is the change in deviance between the null random effects logit panel model (i.e. the model that includes only the constant) and the full model. In this example this is $(-2*(-713.46565))$ $- (-2*(-622.63259)) = 181.67$. The model has 3 degrees of freedom and therefore the LR chi2 test is significant and can be interpreted as it would in a cross-sectional logit model (or as an F test would be in a standard regression model).

The next panel of the output in Figure 44 is similar to the regression information in a standard cross-sectional logit model. Coefficients are presented along with their standard errors, a z test and the upper and lower bounds of a 95 per cent confidence interval.

In the final part of the output Figure 44 provides information about the 'panel-level' variance component. This is displayed as */lnsig2u*, which is the log *of sigma_u²*. The standard deviation of the variance *sigma_u* is also displayed. In the random effects logit panel model the total variance can be considered as $(sigma\_u)^2 + (sigma\_e)^2$; however, *sigma_e* is not

```
Random-effects logistic regression          Number of obs      =      1,580
Group variable: case                        Number of groups   =        155

Random effects u_i ~ Gaussian               Obs per group:
                                                         min =          1
                                                         avg =       10.2
                                                         max =         14

Integration method: mvaghermite             Integration pts.   =         12

                                            LR chi2(3)         =     181.67
Log likelihood  = -622.63259                Prob > chi2        =     0.0000

------------------------------------------------------------------------------
     femp |     Coef.   Std. Err.      z    P>|z|     [95% Conf. Interval]
----------+-------------------------------------------------------------------
   1.mune |  -2.695256   .4843283    -5.56   0.000    -3.644522    -1.74599
   1.und5 |  -2.499021   .2427658   -10.29   0.000    -2.974833   -2.023209
   regage |   .0331013   .0193458     1.71   0.087    -.0048157    .0710183
    _cons |   1.480233   .4275885     3.46   0.001     .6421746    2.318291
----------+-------------------------------------------------------------------
 /lnsig2u |   2.043738   .2025732                      1.646702    2.440774
----------+-------------------------------------------------------------------
  sigma_u |   2.778382    .281413                      2.278121    3.388499
      rho |   .7011731    .042445                      .6120302    .7772872
------------------------------------------------------------------------------
LR test of rho=0: chibar2(01) = 511.52                Prob >= chibar2 = 0.000
```

Figure 44 Stata output: Random effects logit panel model wife employed

reported in the output because it is fixed at $\pi^2/3$. Rho can be considered as the proportion of variance that can be attributed to the panel and can be calculated using Stata's *display* command:

display (e(sigma_u)^2)/(3.29 +(e(sigma_u)^2))

Rho = 0.70 in this example, which is the proportion of the variance that is due to u_i. The 95 per cent confidence interval for rho is 0.61, 0.78. There is a formal LR test that rho = 0. This test formally compares the pooled cross-sectional logit model with the random effects logit panel model. The LR ch2 value is the Deviance$_{pooled\_logit\_model}$ – Deviance$_{random\_effects\_model}$. In this example $(-2* -878.39) - (-2*-622.63)$. More generally, this information can be recovered in Stata using the two scalars that store these values, using the following Stata syntax:

display (-2(e(ll_c))) - (-2*(e(ll)))*

The LR ch2 value 511.52 is significant at 1 degree of freedom (p < 0.001). The extra degree of freedom reflects the extra parameter in the panel model that is represented by the random effect.

We now turn our attention to estimating the fixed effects logit panel model. This model can be estimated using the following Stata syntax:

xtlogit femp i.mune i.und5 regage, fe

The results of the fixed effects logit panel model are reported in Figure 45. Stata reports a very important piece of information – 'multiple positive outcomes within groups encountered'. Seventy-two wives have been dropped from the model. This is because these women have been either employed (*femp==1*) or not employed (*femp==0*) in all of the waves in which they were observed. In practice this fixed effects logit panel model is estimated on only 83 women (who have changed states during the life of the panel). This is a major restriction of the fixed effects logit panel model, which we will return to later. For the moment it is worth remembering that the fixed effects logit panel model and random effects logit panel model are not directly comparable unlike the standard fixed effects panel model and random effects model that are used to analyse a continuous outcome. The model analyses 949 rows of data from 83 wives. The minimum number of observations is 2, the maximum number of observations is 14 and the average number of observations is 11.4.

```
note: multiple positive outcomes within groups encountered.
note: 72 groups (631 obs) dropped because of all positive or
      all negative outcomes.

Iteration 0:   log likelihood = -325.88392
Iteration 1:   log likelihood = -317.86118
Iteration 2:   log likelihood = -317.84572
Iteration 3:   log likelihood = -317.84572

Conditional fixed-effects logistic regression    Number of obs   =       949
Group variable: case                             Number of groups =        83

                                                 Obs per group:
                                                            min =         2
                                                            avg =      11.4
                                                            max =        14

                                                 LR chi2(3)      =    134.08
Log likelihood = -317.84572                      Prob > chi2     =    0.0000

------------------------------------------------------------------------------
      femp |      Coef.   Std. Err.      z    P>|z|     [95% Conf. Interval]
-----------+------------------------------------------------------------------
    1.mune | -2.484055   .5537771    -4.49   0.000    -3.569438   -1.398671
    1.und5 | -2.256592   .2434573    -9.27   0.000    -2.733759   -1.779424
    regage |  .0456201   .0246289     1.85   0.064    -.0026517    .093892
------------------------------------------------------------------------------
```

Figure 45 Stata output: Fixed effects logit panel model wife employed

The LR chi2 is the Deviance$_{null\_fixed\_effects\_model}$ – Deviance$_{full\_fixed\_effects\_model}$' which can be recovered from the scalar variables after the model is estimated:

display (–2* e(ll_0)) – (–2* e(ll))

The LR chi2 is significant at 3 degrees of freedom and it can be interpreted as an overall assessment of the model (i.e. as an *F* test would be in a standard regression model).

The fixed effects logit panel model is also known as a 'conditional logistic regression' and this terminology is reported in the Stata output. The model can also be estimated with Stata's *clogit* command. The results are identical, but the *clogit* model emerges from a different analytical area. Historically, conditional logistic regression models were used for matched case-control data (see McFadden, 1973). The conditional logistic regression model is well suited to research data with matched pairs, for example. The fixed effects logit panel model is not especially well suited to many panel datasets where the respondents remain in a single state, because these cases are inevitably dropped from the analysis.

Logistic regression models are commonly used in the analysis of large-scale datasets in social science disciplines such as sociology and social policy, but by contrast the probit model is ubiquitous within economics. These two approaches are special cases within the broader generalized linear modelling (glm) framework (see Nelder and Wedderburn, 1972). In our experience these two models are so sufficiently similar that they will usually lead to nearly identical substantive conclusions. An understanding of both approaches for modelling binary outcomes is useful and can open up possibilities with more specialized models.

Coefficients from a pooled cross-sectional logit model and a pooled cross-sectional probit model are reported in Table 9. Amemiya (1981)

Table 9 Coefficients for the pooled regression models wife employed (logit and probit models)

	β_{logit}	$\beta_{logit}/1.6$	β_{probit}	$\beta_{probit}{}^{*}1.6$
mune	−1.71	−1.07	−1.01	−1.62
und5	−1.79	−1.12	−1.09	−1.74
regage	−0.01	0.00	0.00	−0.01
constant	1.42	0.89	0.87	1.39

proposes a simple transformation of estimates between logit and probit models of 1.6. Therefore, $\beta_{logit} = (\beta_{probit} * 1.6)$ and $\beta_{probit} = (\beta_{logit}/1.6)$. The estimates of β_{logit} and β_{probit} usually do not map onto each other completely. Therefore, there will usually be very minor differences, for example when predicted probabilities are calculated, but these differences are not usually a case for alarm.

Aldrich and Nelson (1984) suggest an alternative scaling factor of $\pi/\sqrt{3}$ = 1.814. Liao (1994) asserts that the most accurate value of the conversion factor lies somewhere in the neighbourhood of these two proposed values. He further asserts that there could be analyses where the logit and probit results differ substantially, for example when there are an extremely large number of observations heavily concentrated in the tails of the distribution. In these rare circumstances, we would advise data analysts to place extra thought into which form of glm they estimate given the specific research question and available data, and not to simply be guided by their own disciplinary traditions.

A random effects probit panel model can be estimated in Stata with the following syntax:

xtprobit femp i.mune i.und5 regage, re noskip

Stata reports almost identical information after estimating the random effects probit panel model *xtprobit* and the random effects logit panel model *xtlogit* (compare Figure 46 with Figure 44). The main difference is that *xtprobit* coefficients are calculated using the cumulative distribution function of the standard normal distribution. A further difference between the *xtlogit* model and the *xtprobit* model is that rho is calculated slightly differently. In the random effects probit panel model the total variance can be considered as $(sigma\_u)^2 + (sigma\_e)^2$, but *sigma_e* is not reported in the output because it is fixed at 1 (rather than at $\pi^2 / 3$ as it is in the random effects logit panel model). The value of rho for the random effects probit panel model can be calculated manually in Stata

display (e(sigma_u)^2)/((e(sigma_u)^2)+1)

There is no command in Stata for a fixed effects probit panel model. This is because the probit distribution does not provide a 'sufficient statistic' that can be used in the modelling process (a technical account of this issue is provided in Greene and Hensher, 2010).

```
Random-effects probit regression          Number of obs     =      1,580
Group variable: case                      Number of groups  =        155

Random effects u_i ~ Gaussian             Obs per group:
                                                        min =          1
                                                        avg =       10.2
                                                        max =         14

Integration method: mvaghermite           Integration pts.  =         12

                                          LR chi2(3)        =     176.86
Log likelihood  = -624.58689              Prob > chi2       =     0.0000

-----------------------------------------------------------------------------
      femp |      Coef.   Std. Err.      z    P>|z|     [95% Conf. Interval]
-----------+-----------------------------------------------------------------
    1.mune |  -1.415054   .2563382    -5.52   0.000    -1.917468   -.9126404
    1.und5 |  -1.380961    .130322   -10.60   0.000    -1.636388   -1.125535
    regage |   .0179768   .0107089     1.68   0.093    -.0030123    .0389658
     _cons |   .8141995   .2372817     3.43   0.001      .349136    1.279263
-----------+-----------------------------------------------------------------
  /lnsig2u |   .8774007   .1965582                       .4921538    1.262648
-----------+-----------------------------------------------------------------
   sigma_u |   1.550691   .1524005                       1.278998    1.880098
       rho |   .7062833   .0407754                       .6206137    .7794816
-----------------------------------------------------------------------------
LR test of rho=0: chibar2(01) = 507.92             Prob >= chibar2 = 0.000
```

Figure 46 Stata output: Random effects probit panel model

Marginal effects for the random effects probit panel model (Figure 46) are reported in Figure 47. The predicted probability of a wife being employed if her husband was unemployed is 0.25 compared with 0.77 if her husband was employed. The predicted probability of a wife being employed if she had a child under age 5 was 0.36 compared with 0.85 if she did not have a child under age 5. These predictions are made holding the woman's age at 36. This might at first appear confusing but the predictions are made at the mean of the variable *regage*, which is 18.01. The variable *regage* is the women's age in years minus 18 because the variable age was centred in the data.

An important part of the Stata output is that $Pr(femp=1$ assuming $u\_i=0)$; this reminds us that the prediction that the outcome variable equals 1 (in this case $femp==1$) is made on the assumption that $u\_i=0$ (or expressed another way the panel-level variance is zero). We advise that these marginal estimates should be considered as being indicative and useful for illustrative purposes rather than being thought of as more solid estimates of probability. On this topic Stewart (2006) offers further advice and states that care must be taken when comparing coefficients from random effects probit models and pooled probit models. This is because

```
Adjusted predictions                          Number of obs    =      1,580
Model VCE    : OIM

Expression   : Pr(femp=1 assuming u_i=0), predict(pu0)
at           : 0.mune          =     .9259494  (mean)
               1.mune          =     .0740506  (mean)
               0.und5          =     .7025316  (mean)
               1.und5          =     .2974684  (mean)
               regage          =     18.01013  (mean)

------------------------------------------------------------------------------
             |            Delta-method
             |    Margin   Std. Err.      z    P>|z|     [95% Conf. Interval]
-------------+----------------------------------------------------------------
        mune |
           0 |   .7664395   .0445551    17.20   0.000     .6791132    .8537658
           1 |   .2457633   .0859617     2.86   0.004     .0772815    .4142451
             |
        und5 |
           0 |   .8492397   .0351396    24.17   0.000     .7803673     .918112
           1 |   .3640015   .0627663     5.80   0.000     .2409819    .4870211
------------------------------------------------------------------------------
```

Figure 47 Stata output: Margins (adjusted predictions at means) for the random effects probit model wife employed presented in Figure 46

the models use different normalizations. The practical solution that he proposes is to multiply $\beta_{\text{random\_effects}}$ by $\sqrt{1 - rho}$.

Panel models with other outcomes

We have argued that panel models should be considered as extensions of cross-sectional regression models. So far we have limited our discussion to the analysis of continuous and binary outcomes. Just as there are a range of models designed to analyse other types of outcomes in cross-sectional data there are also a range of alternative panel models. Many of these models can easily be estimated in Stata.

The *xtologit* command fits random effects ordered logistic regression panel models, and *xtoprobit* fits random effects ordered probit regression panel models. A complementary log-log (cloglog) random effects panel model can be estimated using *xtcloglog*. This model is for a binary dependent variable, and it is typically used when one of the outcomes is rare relative to the other.

In Stata there are a series of models suitable for count data; for example *xtpoisson* can estimate both random effects Poisson panel models and fixed effects Poisson panel models. The negative binomial model can be used for count data with over-dispersion (e.g. with a variance that is larger than the mean) in a panel context with *xtnbreg*. At the time of writing there is no command in Stata for multinomial logit models in a panel context, but a feasible work-around has been suggested.[11] A random effects multinomial logit model can be estimated using the Stata extension program *gllamm* (see Rabe-Hesketh, Skrondal and Pickles, 2004). We anticipate that the *xt* suite is likely to include additional models in the future.

Dynamic panel models

Dynamic panel models are further extensions to the models used to ana-lyse quantitative longitudinal data. Dynamic panel models appeal to the idea of using panel data to better understand 'state dependence'. Lagged dependent variables, for example a measure of Y_{it-1} and Y_{it-2}, are incor-porated as explanatory variables in the model. This is made complicated because the lagged dependent variables will themselves be influenced by unobserved effects. In practice, this will mean that standard panel estima-tion procedures will be inconsistent. Arellano and Bond (1991) derived a suitable estimator which is available using the Stata command *xtabond*.

Economists have highlighted the potential applications for dynamic panel models for some time (see Anderson and Hsiao, 1982; Nickell, 1981), and Arellano and Bond (1991) used a dynamic model to investigate labour demand. Analyses with lagged dependent variables are less common in other areas of social science. In many areas of social science continuous outcome variables are far less common, and models such as *xtabond* have fewer applications. In this section we briefly discuss one example of using dynamic panel models that are suitable for binary outcomes.

Stewart (2006) sets out a dynamic random effects probit panel model. The model can be implemented in Stata as the *redprob* command when the .*ado* file is downloaded from the web.[12] In summary, *redprob* estimates a dynamic probit model in which the outcome probability is dependent on the outcome in the previous time period (e.g. t − 1). The model is espe-cially designed to address the issue of when residual heterogeneity, in the

---

11 See http://www.stata.com/stata-news/news29-2/xtmlogit/ (accessed 25 May 2016).

12 See http://www2.warwick.ac.uk/fac/soc/economics/staff/mstewart/stata (accessed 25 May 2016).

form of individual-specific effects, results in an 'initial conditions' problem which would render the estimates from a standard random effects probit panel model inconsistent. Stewart (2007) uses the *redprob* approach and compares and contrasts it with other possible advanced estimation techniques to evaluate the dynamics of unemployment and low-paid work. Boyle, Feng and Gayle (2009a) use the dynamic random effects probit panel model to explore family migration and female employment using data from the BHPS with additional control for initial conditions.

Considering 'initial conditions' is important in many analyses. Some quantitative longitudinal studies begin collecting data at the start of a social process, for example the older UK birth cohorts all began with babies who were born in one week. Similarly the Youth Cohort Study of England and Wales follows a cohort who are all eligible to leave full-time education at the same point in time. In other quantitative longitudinal studies, for example most household panel studies, data collection interrupts ongoing social processes. In these situations, the initial response is typically related to circumstances that predate data collection, and this is often referred to as the 'initial conditions problem'. It is reasonable to anticipate that as the length of the sequence increases, the effect of the initial condition should weaken. Fotouhi (1990) provides encouraging results from simulations that chime with this idea. The most obvious 'initial conditions problem' arises when there is a lagged response variable, because this outcome is related to the period before the study began (Fotouhi and Davies, 2007). A dynamic model such as *redprob* that explicitly models initial conditions is therefore attractive.

The creation of lagged variables requires some data enabling but it is relatively straightforward in Stata. For example, in a long format dataset (i.e. with individual observations stacked up wave on wave), a lagged Y variable (*lag1y*) can be created with the following Stata syntax:

    sort id wave
    gen lag1y = y[_n-1] if id==id[_n-1]

or alternatively

    bysort id: gen lag1y = y[_n-1]

Stata also has the facility to automatically create and use what are known as *time-series* variables. For example, *L.gnp* refers to the lagged value of variable *gnp*. In practice we advise analysts to be careful when constructing lagged variables. This is because panels are seldom perfectly balanced and there will often be gaps in the data, for example missing waves. The example code above will simply match the last recorded value for a given respondent. If the respondent didn't contribute to the previous wave, the data might actually refer to their value from two waves ago.

Estimating random effects models in Stata

In this chapter we have concentrated on models that are estimated using Stata's *xt* suite. In Stata the random effects panel model can also be estimated in the suite *mixed*. This suite of commands estimates identical models but uses alternative syntax, which draws on different terminology because it is orientated towards working within a multilevel modelling framework. In practice, model results from the *mixed* and *xt* suites may initially differ slightly because Stata uses alternative default settings. Stata is very flexible and users can easily re-specify models.

Conclusions

There are many different approaches that can be used to analyse repeated contacts data, including some which use fairly standard modelling techniques and others which make use of additional parameters and assumptions to capture the complexity of the data structure. Most statistical models that are used for panel data fall into the class of 'generalized linear mixed models' (Hedeker, 2005). This means that they can be used for linear and non-linear outcomes, and they can accommodate terms that help recognize how individuals make multiple contributions to the dataset. There are two particularly important classes of panel model. The first includes models that use 'fixed effects' and include more explicit (i.e. 'fixed') parameters for individuals. The second class includes models that use 'random effects' and model patterns in the error distribution associated with individuals. There are also numerous interesting extensions to standard panel models, such as dynamic panel models that incorporate lagged information on outcomes or explanatory variables.

At least three distinctive methodological literatures can be identified that are orientated towards the analysis of repeated contacts data. The first emerges from econometrics where the analysis of panel datasets is common (Baum, 2006). The econometrics tradition has probably been the most influential in shaping the approaches taken by other social science disciplines (Allison, 2009; Dale and Davies, 1994; Treiman, 2009). A second methodological tradition emerges from public health and the study of disease where observational studies often include repeated contacts data. This has led to methodological developments of panel data analysis in epidemiology and biostatistics (Suárez et al., 2016; Rabe-Hesketh and Skrondal, 2012).

A third literature can also be identified, which is concerned with random effects models and is generally termed as 'multilevel modelling' (see Goldstein, 2011), but is sometimes called 'hierarchical linear modelling' (Raudenbush and Bryk, 2002). The substantive focus of the multilevel modelling literature has often been the hierarchical clustering of non-panel datasets, such as of pupils within classrooms in educational research. Conceptually, multilevel modelling is also an appropriate approach for the panel data, when multiple observations (e.g. yearly personal interviews in a household panel study) are clustered within the same observational unit (i.e. the adult respondent in the survey).

There is a great deal of overlap in the statistical data analysis techniques that are covered by the methodological literatures associated with these three traditions. There is some divergence in the specific approaches that are advocated and obvious differences in the topics and format of the research examples that are used. In econometrics, for instance, the 'fixed effects' panel model is often presented as the preferable solution, whereas in the epidemiological and multilevel modelling traditions, various forms of 'random effects' models are more commonly endorsed. Unfortunately, the terminology used in these three methodological areas is usually quite different. In our experience this frequently leads to confusion, especially for researchers who are new to the analysis of repeated contacts data. Because the focus of the book is large-scale quantitative longitudinal social science datasets, we have generally adopted the terminology most commonly used in the panel data analysis literature, which emerges from econometrics. Nevertheless, it is useful to be aware of all three traditions, not least because published research projects can draw upon the terminology used in any one of these literatures, and technical language from each intellectual tradition is often used interchangeably.

6 Adopting the long view: A review of analytical methods

The main message

In the absence of data with a temporal dimension there is little that can reliably be concluded regarding social change or social stability. For many research questions cross-sectional data will be sufficient, but the answers to most research questions can be valuably enhanced with the addition of some longitudinal data analyses. Some questions can only be sensibly and comprehensively answered using longitudinal data.

The generality and flexibility of large-scale longitudinal data resources facilitates their use in a wide variety of circumstances. Repeated cross-sectional surveys often provide useful sources of information, particularly when the main research focus is describing longer term social trends. Cohort studies tend to be well suited to the study of growth or development in specific contexts. Cross-cohort comparisons are especially effective when the research focus is investigating generational differences. Household panel studies usually collect a broad spectrum of data, and they tend to be suited to studying micro-level social change especially over shorter time periods. Sometimes it is also possible to construct pseudo-cohorts from household panel studies to study growth or development.

There are a number of methodological benefits to using repeated contacts data in social science research. Repeated contacts data provide detailed information on transitions and changes experienced by individuals, and they ensure that researchers accurately disentangle the temporal ordering of events by charting exactly how events unfold in the individual's lifecourse. Repeated contacts data also support the estimation of statistical models that provide improved control for residual heterogeneity (or omitted explanatory variables). Residual heterogeneity is almost inevitable because within analyses some important variables will not have been included, either because the measure was not available or because it was not possible to measure it in a survey context. There is a frequently noted empirical regularity that current behaviour is influenced by previous behaviour. Repeated contacts data allow models to be estimated that explicitly provide improved control for previous behaviour (state dependence).

Using existing datasets

Longitudinal data are time consuming and expensive to collect and we would always advise researchers to begin by investigating existing longitudinal data resources before embarking on collecting new longitudinal data. There is now a broad portfolio of survey data available to social science researchers. The existing large-scale longitudinal datasets are often 'omnibus' studies that collect hundreds of measures on a broad spectrum of topics.

A large-scale longitudinal data resource might not have exactly the variable that a researcher is looking for to undertake a particular analysis. In these circumstances it is often good advice to compromise a little and we would advise the researcher to think hard about what they wish to achieve. For example, imagine a situation where one option is to use a variable from the BHPS that is less than fully optimal. Another option is to begin a new data collection exercise attempting to collect a more appropriate or optimal variable. The BHPS provides nearly two decades of systematically collected data on a very large sample of individuals and households. Measures within the BHPS are robust and their reliability and validity have been investigated and tested. In this example there seems little contest. This is not to argue that large-scale social surveys are a 'data panacea' for all research questions, but they should be preferred whenever they provide relevant data.

Statistical models for quantitative longitudinal analyses

The known universe of statistical techniques is constantly expanding, and the array of techniques may seem bewildering even for more experienced researchers. It is valuable to have a broad understanding of the most important data analytical options, and in our review we have discussed some of the most prominent approaches to longitudinal data analysis in the social sciences. It is good advice not to stray too far from established conventions. Our observation is that many of the most successful applied social researchers are relatively pragmatic in their use of statistical methods and focus on those approaches with a tradition of relevance to their own field of social science research. There are always new and emergent ideas in social statistics, but some of the more esoteric developments may not provide a suitable intellectual return on the outlay of erudition required to gain sufficient expertise to apply them.

The positive message is that most researchers undertaking longitudinal data analysis with large-scale social science datasets will use a core of techniques that shelter under the umbrella term 'generalized linear mixed models' (glmm). The positive message is that these models are the natural extensions of models in the generalized linear model (glm) family (which include standard regression models and logistic regression models). Models within the glmm family are flexible enough to be well suited to an enormous range of empirical research questions using longitudinal social science data.

The technical work outlined in Clark and Linzer (2015) and Bell and Jones (2015) provides persuasive methodological evidence of the flexibility and generality of random effects panel models from the glmm family. For many social science research questions where large-scale repeated contacts data are used, a random effects panel modelling approach will probably be adequate because of its generality. There are also many scenarios where the fixed effects panel model is more compelling. A strong account of the statistical foundations of panel models and their application in social science research is provided by Halaby (2004). Researchers requiring further practical advice on estimating panel models using Stata should consult Longhi and Nandi (2014).

Recent advances in estimating generalized linear mixed models mean that increasingly they can also incorporate information on the design of complex social surveys (e.g. clustering, stratification and sampling weights). Many models can be conveniently estimated using Stata's *meglm* suite, which estimates multilevel mixed-effects generalized linear models and can be combined with the *svy* suite.[1] This brings together two previously disparate advanced statistical areas that are potentially pertinent to the analysis of the BHPS, the UKHLS and the MCS, all of which have

---

1 A brief overview and a succinct example are provided on the Stata website http://www.stata.com/new-in-stata/multilevel-models-survey-data/ (accessed 24 June 2016).

complex designs (see Taylor et al., 2010; Lynn, 2009b; Lynn and Kaminska, 2010; Ketende and Jones, 2011a).

Further methodological issues

This book is part of the *What Is* series that focuses on introducing readers to new methodological areas. Due to its orientation and length there are a number of more advanced topics that have been strategically omitted. These topics include the estimation and interpretation of interaction effects in statistical models (see Ai and Norton, 2003; Norton, Wang and Ai, 2004; Mitchell and Chen, 2005), post-estimation measures and model evaluation (see Long and Freese, 2014) and missing data (see Carpenter and Kenward, 2012). A range of advanced methodological issues relating specifically to quantitative longitudinal social surveys (e.g. sample attrition, panel conditioning, interviewer effects and data collection modes) are also not covered (see Lynn, 2009a).

Speculation on the future of longitudinal social science datasets and other emerging resources

An emerging area that we are confident to speculate upon is administrative social science data. Administrative data are records and information that are gathered in order to organize, manage or deliver a service (Elias, 2014). Although they are not primarily collected for research, some administrative data resources contain information that has great potential for longitudinal social research. Historically, social scientists have had very limited access to administrative data, but there is increasing pressure to improve its availability. In the UK, initiatives such as the Economic and Social Research Council (ESRC) funded Administrative Data Research Network[2] seek to improve access to data that are routinely collected by government departments and other agencies. Administrative social science datasets often have a temporal aspect and repeated observations are made on the same units (e.g. individuals, households, schools etc.). This makes them suitable for longitudinal analyses. Administrative datasets are not the product of systematic social science data collection activities, rather they

---

2 See http://www.adrn.ac.uk/ (accessed 6 June 2016).

are the by-product of some other process (see Harford, 2014; Connelly et al., 2016c). Therefore, administrative social science data tend to be far messier than other social science datasets that are specifically collected and then curated to facilitate research.

In comparison with large-scale social surveys, especially omnibus surveys such as the UKHLS, which are specifically designed to support multidisciplinary data analyses, the number of available explanatory variables in most administrative datasets is extremely limited. For example, variables measuring a person's ethnicity or level of education, which are key variables in many analyses, might be completely absent in a dataset because they are irrelevant for the administrative process that the data are collected for.

Administrative data offers great potential for social science research, but our view is that it is likely to prove most effective when linked to well-designed longitudinal studies. Progress is already being made and a range of administrative sources including welfare benefits, health and education have been linked to some large-scale surveys (Sala, Burton and Knies, 2012). The UKHLS has already linked administrative data and there are plans to include further administrative data on education, health, economic circumstances and transport, and data on other topics are likely to be included in the future. In the longer term the UKHLS is also likely to be enriched by the collection of a range of data that go beyond the constraints of the standard survey interview. These activities may include using the survey as a sampling frame for qualitative longitudinal research, using diary methods to collect information (e.g. on time use) and developing experiments (Buck and McFall, 2012). Ermisch et al. (2009) provide an interesting example of an experimental design on trust that was developed using a sampling frame of households that were formerly members of the BHPS.

Some methodologists have suggested that the increasing use of administrative data and 'big data' more generally might lead to a transcendence in methods of statistical analysis (Playford et al., 2016). There is absolutely nothing that convinces us that a longitudinal analysis drawing upon administrative data should ignore the important lessons that have emerged from many decades of research into longitudinal analytical methods in social statistics and statistically orientated areas of social science such as econometrics.

A new phase in quantitative longitudinal social surveys is the collection of biomeasures (which are also referred to as biomarkers). The main motivation for the collection of these measures in surveys such as the UKHLS is to augment survey data with objective health measures and genetic information to better support investigations of biological and environmental influences on human behaviour and health (McFall et al., 2012). Further information on the collection of biomeasures in the UKHLS is provided in McFall, Conolly and Burton (2014), and Davillas et al. (2016) is one empirical research example using these data. Biomeasures have also been included in major longitudinal studies such as the ELSA (see Read and Grundy, 2012) and the NCDS (1958 birth cohort) (see Calvin et al., 2011).

The UK has an impressive set of large-scale birth cohort studies with national coverage. The birth cohort studies support a wide range of analyses associated with development and change (or stability) over the lifecourse. The Life Study was the name given to the next UK birth cohort study which aimed to recruit babies born between 2014 and 2018. In October 2015 the UK ESRC and the UK MRC agreed that funding for the Life Study was discontinued due to the serious challenges encountered in recruiting participants.[3] The future of the existing UK birth cohort studies appears to be secure at the present time, but the establishment of further new cohort studies is currently unclear.

Conclusions

Quantitative longitudinal data analysis is essential for researchers who are serious about providing comprehensive answers to research questions that require, or would benefit from, a longitudinal perspective. The analysis of appropriate quantitative longitudinal data will provide intellectual returns for the extra analytical efforts that inevitably are required. On many occasions we have found quantitative longitudinal data analysis to be an all-absorbing activity, and sometimes it has even been enjoyable. Nevertheless, the endeavour itself is not without its challenges, and Angrist and Pischke (2008) playfully remarked that if applied research was easy then theorists would do it. They also reassure readers that applied research is not as hard as the dense pages of *Econometrica* might lead us to believe.

Some of the challenges of analysing longitudinal data lie with the complex array of data analysis techniques through which we have tried to

---

3 See http://www.lifestudy.ac.uk/about/faqs (accessed 24 June 2016).

navigate in the preceding pages. Many of the challenges relate to issues of organizing and understanding data and preparing it for subsequent analysis (i.e. 'enabling data'). Quantitative longitudinal social science data are messy and confusing, and that is because the contemporary social world is messy and confusing. The deeper you dig into quantitative longitudinal data, the more tricky and bewildering it becomes. This need not be a permanent or insoluble state and given a little time and modest effort it is possible for researchers to increase their understanding of a dataset.

The skills required for enabling data, managing the workflow and undertaking longitudinal data analyses are initially perplexing. In the closing chapter we hope to assist readers who want to start analysing longitudinal data, primarily by focusing on the practical issues of enabling and preparing complex datasets for analyses.

7 Getting started

The preceding chapters have set out 'what is' longitudinal data analysis. This final chapter is more practical and outlines 'how to begin to undertake' longitudinal data analysis. It is envisioned as an aid to making a smooth departure on the journey of longitudinal research, and it is not intended to be a comprehensive guide to undertaking data analyses.

It is infeasible to attempt longitudinal social science data analysis without using data analysis software. Several statistical data analysis packages are available to social science researchers. The three that are currently most prevalent are SPSS, Stata and R. We advocate using Stata for longitudinal data analysis, and a justification for this preference is outlined in Gayle and Lambert (2017). Researchers are of course free to use whichever software they prefer.

The workflow

Software can be operated in different ways, but the complexity of longitudinal datasets means that nearly all highly skilled researchers write out software commands using a syntactical or programming format, which in turn forms an audit trail. The audit trail is a central aspect of the workflow, which includes planning, organizing, executing and documenting analyses.

We advise all readers to consult Gayle and Lambert (2017), which provides detailed prescriptions on the social science data analysis workflow, and we are fairly certain that it will help most researchers regardless of how much experience they have analysing social survey data. A more wide-ranging account of the workflow is set out by Long (2009), and in our view Long is the definitive text on this subject. In Gayle and Lambert (2017) we treat a number of highly important practical issues that are usually overlooked in data analysis texts. These topics include organizing directory structures, adopting file-naming conventions, keeping track of files (i.e. version control), managing variables, and structuring and documenting software syntax files.

Documentation is fundamental to achieving a workflow that is accurate, efficient and transparent, and which facilitates reproduction. Long (2009) posits Long's law, which states that it is easier to document today than it is tomorrow. He further states that there are two corollaries. First, nobody likes to write documentation. Second, nobody ever regrets writing documentation. We suggest that in the history of social survey data analysis, no one has ever said 'This work is too well documented'. We encourage longitudinal data analysts to make frequent notes and comments because these will be the backbone of documentation.

Analysing longitudinal data without a planned and organized workflow can be compared to drinking and driving. In both situations, no matter how careful you are, it is still highly likely to end in a wreck![1] Therefore, just like drinking and driving, we strongly warn against not having a systematic workflow and in our view no researcher should ever undertake any serious survey data analyses without a planned and organized workflow.

Data enabling

Social surveys almost always require some preparatory work before analyses can be undertaken. We use the term 'data enabling' to describe this phase of the workflow. In reality, even appropriately curated social science datasets will require some work to be undertaken to enable data analyses, even if only recoding some variables or coding some missing values.

Longitudinal datasets are almost never provided in a form that renders them immediately ready for comprehensive analyses. Social scientists face many practical difficulties when enabling longitudinal data for analyses. The most obvious challenge is linking up individuals at multiple time points. Less obvious are the difficulties associated with matching individuals with others in the study, for example spouses, children, siblings or other household sharers. Many research questions also require the addition of

---

1 We are grateful to Professor Philip Stark, University of California Berkeley, for this useful and clear analogy.

important contextual information, for example about the household or locality, which can also prove challenging.

A substantial but often under-appreciated aspect of working with longitudinal datasets is the challenge of constructing appropriate measures which aid comparability over time or which suitably reflect social changes. There are often a number of different measures (e.g. different socio-economic classifications) in the dataset that could be used, and often metadata are also supplied with the dataset. A weakness of some analyses is that they do not take full advantage of the richer data resources available in the survey because they are restricted to exploiting only the most readily available information.

Over the course of our careers we have learnt the important lesson that the process of data enabling usually takes five times as long as initially anticipated. Data enabling tasks that researchers initially think will take an hour usually take five hours, and similarly tasks that we think will take a day end up taking five days. This is an important lesson to internalize, and our advice is to try to ensure that you build in adequate time for enabling your data and try to remember that data enabling tasks are usually very time consuming. Our graduate students refer to the idea of 'five times' as the 'Gayle-Lambert constant'. We prefer to think of it as a guideline because there will undoubtedly be social scientists with better programming skills than ours, who can work faster and program more efficiently.

Using Stata

In our view the software Stata is particularly well suited for the combined tasks of data enabling and data analysis that characterize longitudinal social science data analysis. There are many resources aimed at providing Stata training. We recommend Kohler and Kreuter (2012) and Mehmetoglu and Jakobsen (2016) because they are well-organized and informative texts. Some students prefer Pevalin and Robson (2009). We also recommend Treiman (2009), which is an excellent text covering a wider range of advanced topics and issues that researchers are likely to encounter. We enthusiastically promote the Institute for Digital Research and Education (IDRE), University of California, Los Angeles, web resources[2] and draw

---

2 See https://idre.ucla.edu/ (accessed 6 April 2016).

attention to their Stata pages[3] and very helpful annotated outputs pages which contain example programs and outputs with footnotes explaining the meaning of information, measures and statistical tests reported in Stata outputs.[4]

As new versions of Stata emerge, commands tend to remain consistent, but occasionally there are changes and some features are no longer supported. The *version* command is a valuable tool in Stata. It ensures that older material (which is sometimes outdated) can be run by newer versions of Stata. For example, the command *version 12* will make Stata version 14 behave as if it were Stata version 12. It is possible that in the future some of the material provided in this book will be incompatible with future versions of Stata and this command may be useful. If you are working in a collaborative project with colleagues that have older versions of Stata, it is often good practice to save files using Stata's *saveold* command.

A benefit of Stata is that new commands and functions are often developed, which can be incorporated into your current version of Stata. It is possible to acquire and manage downloads from the internet using the command *net*. The *findit* command can be used to search the Stata site and other sites for information. For example, imagine that you heard about a program to draw graphs using quasi-variance estimates. Using the syntax *findit qvgraph* would lead you to the module written by Aspen Chen of the University of Connecticut.

Many new packages are deposited at the Statistical Software Components (SSC) archive, which is sometimes called the Boston College Archive and is administered by http://repec.org.[5] The SSC archive has become the premier Stata download site for user-written software and also archives the proceedings of Stata Users Group meetings and conferences. Programs can be downloaded from the SSC archive using the syntax *ssc install* followed by the new program's name. Readers who do not have administrative access to Stata (e.g. when working on their university network) may first require permission to download packages.

---

3 See http://www.ats.ucla.edu/stat/stata/ (accessed 6 April 2016).

4 See http://www.ats.ucla.edu/stat/AnnotatedOutput/ (accessed 6 April 2016).

5 Accessed (12 June 2016).

An alternative approach may be to set up an area locally where you have write access (e.g. c:\temp) and then use a variant of the following Stata syntax:

> *global path10 "c:\temp\"*
> *capture mkdir $path10\stata*
> *capture mkdir $path10\stata\ado*
> *adopath + $path10\stata\ado*
> *net set ado $path10\stata\ado*

You can test this by installing the *estout* package from SSC:

> *ssc install estout*

Help on this new package should then be available:

> *help estout*

Longitudinal data structures in Stata

Most researchers who are used to working with social surveys will be familiar with datasets that are 'variable by case' matrices. The dataset will usually be composed of many rows, each containing information on a single unit (e.g. an individual). It will also be composed of a set of columns. Each column will usually contain information for a single variable. A simple example is illustrated in Figure 48.

Sometimes longitudinal datasets are constructed in 'wide format'. In wide format each row of data represents a single unit, such as a respondent, but some or all of the variables are measures about the unit from different time points. A common strategy is to label relevant variables with

id	Age	female	working_hours
001	20	0	37
002	30	1	39
003	40	1	45

Figure 48 An example of variable by case matrix

a prefix or suffix that indicates the time point that it relates to. A simple example is illustrated in Figure 49. As we discussed earlier there are some longitudinal techniques that require the data to be organized in wide format (e.g. some duration models).

There are other data analysis techniques, for example the panel models that we introduced in Chapter 5, that require data to be organized in 'long format'. In long format, units such as individuals can contribute multiple rows of data, each for a different time period. For example, the wide format dataset that was outlined in Figure 49 can be reorganized into long format, as displayed in Figure 50. The columns of data are no longer specific to different time periods; however, it is important that the dataset contains a variable indicating which time period the row relates to. In Figure 50, this information can be found in the variables *wave* and *year*, which represent the survey wave and the calendar time.

Many longitudinal studies provide information in different data files for different time periods. For example, the main body of the BHPS is supplied as a collection of 18 files for the data collected from adult respondents in

id	female	age_1971	age_1972	age_1973	work_hours_1971	work_hours_1972	work_hours_1973
001	0	20	21	22	37	40	35
002	1	30	31	32	39	40	35
003	1	40	41	42	45	45	15

Figure 49 An example of a wide format dataset

id	wave	year	female	age	work_hours
001	1	1970	0	20	37
001	2	1971	0	21	40
001	3	1972	0	22	35
002	1	1970	1	30	39
002	2	1971	1	31	40
002	3	1972	1	32	35
003	1	1970	1	40	45
003	2	1971	1	41	45
003	3	1972	1	42	15

Figure 50 An example of a long format dataset

each of the 18 years of the survey (known as wave 'a' through to wave 'r'). Usually, if a long format dataset is required, the researcher will open up each file from each year, extract the data that they need, and then add the files together 'on top of each other'. In Stata, this involves using the *append* command and taking care to store information on individual identifiers and time periods.

If a wide format dataset is required, the researcher opens up each file from each year and extracts relevant information, but then matches together different data from different years based upon shared individual identifier variables (e.g. by using Stata's *merge* command). Figure 51 illustrates some typical Stata syntax that may be used for this process for a scenario where we use the first three years of individual-level data from the BHPS and collate data on current marital status (the variable *mastat*). The syntax takes advantage of some standardized file- and variable-naming conventions used in the BHPS. For instance, the prefix letter for a file indicates the year of the data and the prefix letter for a variable within a file similarly indicates the year that the data applies to. Other large-scale social science datasets often feature similar conventions for file and variable names.

Some researchers make use of the Stata command *reshape*, which is a convenient command that is specifically designed to convert longitudinal datasets from wide format to long format and vice versa. The are several useful examples using the *reshape* command in the Stata manual and there is an extended account in Chapter 8 of Mitchell (2010). We generally do not use the *reshape* command in our own work as we tend not to have to move frequently between the two different formats. We have observed that novice data analysts sometimes get into a tangle using the *reshape* command. This is because there is a small risk of losing track of transformations when moving between data formats. A little more work is required but we believe that in general it is better to construct datasets in either format through a more deliberate (and therefore transparent) set of syntax commands.

It is important to stress that in most research scenarios the sequence of commands used to bring together data from different time periods will be much more complicated than the illustration in Figure 51. There will typically be activities associated with coding, harmonizing and documenting variables and dealing with missing data that will take considerable thought, time and effort. There are few situations in data enabling where the case for careful workflow documentation and the use of syntax and

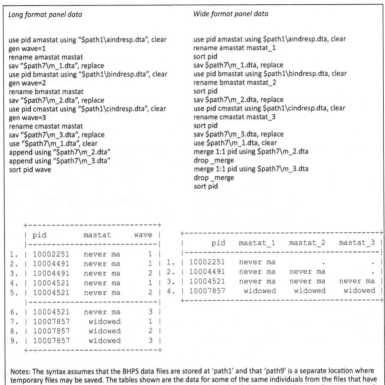

Figure 51 Sample Stata syntax illustrating the construction of long and wide format datasets using the BHPS (and images of the data formats that are generated)

command files is more compelling. A project will run more smoothly if there is a clear and reproducible record of syntax and the steps taken in opening files and processing data from different sources. A longitudinal data analysis project that does not have an organized and systematic workflow with a clear audit trail will be storing up trouble for a later date!

Last words

Oliveira and Stewart (2006) conclude that if your program (in our case the syntax file) is not correct nothing else matters, for without correctness we cannot expect any useful results. Long (2009) reminds us that there is an unavoidable tension between undertaking work carefully and completing work, but he also adds that the production of incorrect results injures both the researcher and the research field.

Using software syntax is central to a well-organized longitudinal data analysis workflow and much of the time spent analysing data involves undertaking repetitive tasks. As Long (2009) helpfully reminds readers, repetition invites errors, and automation which can be achieved through suitably programming software is both faster and less error prone. Developing good data enabling skills pays important dividends because these skills allow researchers to take fuller advantage of the richer data resources available. Good data enabling skills will free researchers from the shackles of having to analyse only the most readily available information. The most obvious payoff for having an effective workflow is that accurate results can be produced systematically and efficiently. Academic life is measured by outputs and structured by deadlines, and an organized workflow can make an essential contribution to making progress.

Data citations

Croxford, L., Iannelli, C., Shapira, M. (2007). *Youth Cohort Time Series for England, Wales and Scotland, 1984-2002*. [data collection]. UK Data Service. SN: 5765, http://dx.doi.org/10.5255/UKDA-SN-5765-1.

University of Essex. Institute for Social and Economic Research. (2010). *British Household Panel Survey: Waves 1-18, 1991-2009*. [data collection]. *7th Edition*. UK Data Service. SN: 5151, http://dx.doi.org/10.5255/UKDA-SN-5151-1.

University of Essex. Institute for Social and Economic Research, NatCen Social Research. (2015). *Understanding Society: Waves 1-5, 2009-2014*. [data collection]. *7th Edition*. UK Data Service. SN: 6614, http://dx.doi.org/10.5255/UKDA-SN-6614-7.

Bibliography

Ai, C. and Norton, E. C. 2003. Interaction terms in logit and probit models. *Economics Letters*, 80(1), 123–9.

Akaike, H. 1974. A new look at the statistical model identification. *IEEE Transactions on Automatic Control*, 19(6), 716–23.

Aldrich, J. H. and Nelson, F. D. 1984. *Linear Probability, Logit, and Probit Models (Vol. 45)*. London Sage.

Allison, P. D. 1984. *Event History Analysis: Regression for Longitudinal Event Data (No. 46)*, Newbury Park, California: Sage.

Allison, P. D. 1990. *Fixed Effects Regression Models*. Thousand Oaks, CA: Sage.

Allison, P. D. 2009. *Fixed Effects Regression Models (Vol. 160)*. Thousand Oaks, California: SAGE Publications.

Allison, P. D. 2010. Survival analysis. In: Hancock, G. R. (ed.) *The Reviewer's Guide to Quantitative Methods in the Social Sciences*. Oxford: Routledge.

Amemiya, T. 1981. Qualitative response models: A survey. *Journal of Economic Literature*, 19(4), 1483–536.

Anderson, S., Boyle, P. and Sharp, C. 2008. *A Scottish Longitudinal Study of Ageing: Scoping Study*. Scottish Government Social Research, December 2008.

Anderson, S., Bradshaw, P., Cunningham-Burley, S., Hayes, F., Jamieson, L., Macgregor, A., Marryat, L. and Wasoff, F. 2007. Growing Up in Scotland: Sweep 1 Overview Report, Edinburgh: Scottish Government.

Anderson, T. W. and Hsiao, C. 1982. Formulation and estimation of dynamic models using panel data. *Journal of Econometrics*, 18(1), 47–82.

Angrist, J. D. and Pischke, J.-S. 2009. *Mostly Harmless Econometrics: An Empiricist's Companion*. Princeton, New Jersey: Princeton University Press.

Arellano, M. and Bond, S. 1991. Some tests of specification for panel data: Monte Carlo evidence and an application to employment equations. *The Review of Economic Studies*, 58(2), 277–97.

Baltagi, B. 2008. *Econometric Analysis of Panel Data*. New York: John Wiley & Sons.

Barry, J., Francis, B. and Davies, R. 1989. SABRE: Software for the analysis of binary recurrent events. *Statistical Modelling*. New York: Springer.

Bartley, M. 1994. Unemployment and ill health: Understanding the relationship. *Journal of Epidemiology and Community Health*, 48(4), 333–7.

Bartley, M. and Plewis, I. 1997. Does health-selective mobility account for socioeconomic differences in health? Evidence from England and Wales, 1971 to 1991. *Journal of Health and Social Behavior*, 38, 376–86.

Bartley, M., Kelly, Y. and Sacker, A. 2012. Early life financial adversity and respiratory function in midlife: A prospective birth cohort study. *American Journal of Epidemiology*, 175(1), 33–42.

Batty, G. D., Morton, S., Campbell, D., Clark, H., Smith, G. D., Hall, M., Macintyre, S. and Leon, D. A. 2004. The Aberdeen Children of the 1950s cohort study: Background, methods and follow-up information on a new resource for the study of life course and intergenerational influences on health. *Paediatric and Perinatal Epidemiology*, 18(3), 221–39.

Baum, C. F. 2006. *An Introduction to Modern Econometrics Using Stata*. College Station, TX: Stata Press.

Bell, A. and Jones, K. 2015. Explaining fixed effects: Random effects modeling of time-series cross-sectional and panel data. *Political Science Research and Methods*, 3(01), 133–53.

Bergman, L. R. and Magnusson, D. 1990. General issues about data quality in longitudinal research. *Data Quality in Longitudinal Research*, 1–31.

Bernardi, F. and Ballarino, G. 2016. *Education, Occupation and Social Origin: A Comparative Analysis of the Transmission of Socio-Economic Inequalities*. Cheltenham: Edward Elgar Publishing.

Berrington, A. and Diamond, I. 2000. Marriage or cohabitation: A competing risks analysis of first-partnership formation among the 1958 British birth cohort. *Journal of the Royal Statistical Society: Series A (Statistics in Society)*, 163(2), 127–51.

Berrington, A., Smith, P. and Sturgis, P. 2006. An overview of methods for the analysis of panel data. National Centre for Research Methods e-Print, http://eprints.ncrm.ac.uk/415/

Berthoud, R., Fumagalli, L., Lynn, P. and Platt, L. 2009. Design of the Understanding Society ethnic minority boost sample. *Institute for Social and Economic Research: Understanding Society Working Paper*, 2.

Blossfeld, H.-P. and Hakim, C. 1997. *Between Equalization and Marginalization: Women Working Part-Time in Europe*. Oxford: Oxford University Press.

Blossfeld, H.-P., Golsch, K. and Rohwer, G. 2007. *Event History Analysis with Stata*. Mahwah, NJ: Lawrence Erlbaum Associates.

Boyd, A., Golding, J., Macleod, J., Lawlor, D. A., Fraser, A., Henderson, J., Molloy, L., Ness, A., Ring, S. and Smith, G. D. 2013. Cohort profile: The 'children of the 90s'—the index offspring of the Avon Longitudinal Study of Parents and Children. *International Journal of Epidemiology*, 42(1), 111–27.

Boyle, P. J., Feng, Z. and Gayle, V. 2009a. A new look at family migration and women's employment status. *Journal of Marriage and Family*, 71(2), 417–31.

Boyle, P. J., Norman, P. and Popham, F. 2009c. Social mobility: Evidence that it can widen health inequalities. *Social Science and Medicine*, 68, 1835–42.

Boyle, P. J., Kulu, H., Cooke, T., Gayle, V. and Mulder, C. H. 2008. Moving and union dissolution. *Demography*, 45(1), 209–22.

Boyle, P. J., Feijten, P., Feng, Z., Hattersley, L., Huang, Z., Nolan, J. and Raab, G. 2009b. Cohort profile: The Scottish longitudinal study (SLS). *International Journal of Epidemiology*, 38(2), 385–92.

Breen, R. (ed.) 2004. *Social Mobility in Europe*. Oxford: Oxford University Press.

Breen, R. and Goldthorpe, J. H. 2001. Class, mobility and merit the experience of two British birth cohorts. *European Sociological Review*, 17(2), 81–101.

Breslow, N. 1970. A generalized Kruskal-Wallis test for comparing K samples subject to unequal patterns of censorship. *Biometrika*, 57, 579–94.

Breslow, N. 1974. Covariance analysis of censored survival data. *Biometrics*, 30 (1), 89–99.

Breusch, T. S. and Pagan, A. R. 1980. The Lagrange multiplier test and its applications to model specification in econometrics. *The Review of Economic Studies*, 47(1), 239–53.

Brown, M. J. and Elliott, J. 2010. Family and household profiles: Comparing the 1958 and 1970 Birth Cohorts. *Twenty-First Century Society*, 5(1), 81–101.

Buck, N. and McFall, S. 2012. Understanding Society: Design overview. *Longitudinal and Life Course Studies*, 3(1), 5–17.

Buck, N., Gershuny, J., Rose, D. and Scott, J. 1994. Changing households: The BHPS 1990 to 1992. Colchester, ESRC Research Centre on Micro-social Change, University of Essex.

Budowski, M., Tillmann, R., Zimmermann, E., Wernli, B., Scherpenzeel, A. and Gabadinho, A. 2001. The Swiss Household Panel 1999–2003: Data for research on micro-social change. *ZUMA Nachrichten*, 25(49), 100–125.

Bukodi, E. and Goldthorpe, J. 2011. Social class returns to higher education: Chances of access to the professional and managerial salariat for men in three British birth cohorts. *Longitudinal and Life Course Studies*, 2(2), 185–201.

Bukodi, E., Goldthorpe, J. H., Waller, L. and Kuha, J. 2015. The mobility problem in Britain: new findings from the analysis of birth cohort data. *The British Journal of Sociology*, 66(1), 93–117.

Burkhauser, R. V. and Lillard, D. R. 2005. The contribution and potential of data harmonization for cross-national comparative research. *Journal of Comparative Policy Analysis*, 7(4), 313–30.

Burkhauser, R. V., Butrica, B. A., Daly, M. C., Lillard, D. R. and Burkhauser, R. V. 2000. The Cross-National Equivalent File.

Burton, J., Laurie, H. and Lynn, P. 2011. Appendix: Understanding society design overview. In: McFall, S. L. and Garrington, C. (eds.). *Understanding Society: Early findings from the first wave of the UK's household longitudinal study*. Colchester: Institute for Social and Economic Research, University of Essex.

Buscha, F. and Sturgis, P. 2015. Declining social mobility? Evidence from five linked Censuses in England and Wales 1971–2011. *British Journal of Sociology*, 1–32.

Butler, N. R. and Bonham, D. G. 1963. *The First report of the 1958 British Perinatal Mortality Survey*. Edinburgh and London: E. & S. Livingstone.

Butler, N. R. and Goldstein, H. 1973. Smoking in Pregnancy and Subsequent Child Development. *Br Med J*, 4(5892), 573–5.

Butler, N. R., Despotidou, S. and Shepherd, P. 1997. 1970 British Cohort Study (BCS70) Ten-year Follow-up (formerly known as the Child Health and Education Study, CHES): A Guide to the BCS 10-Year Data Available at the Economic and Social Research Council Data Archive. Social Statistics Research Unit, City University.

Bynner, J. 1999. New routes to employment: Integration and exclusion. *From Education to Work Cross-National Perspectives*, 65–86.

Bynner, J. and Joshi, H. 2002. Equality and opportunity in education: Evidence from the 1958 and 1970 birth cohort studies. *Oxford Review of Education*, 28(4), 405–25.

Bynner, J. and Parsons, S. 2002. Social exclusion and the transition from school to work: The case of young people not in education, employment, or training (NEET). *Journal of Vocational Behavior*, 60(2), 289–309.

Cable, N., Sacker, A. and Bartley, M. 2008. The effect of employment on psychological health in mid-adulthood: Findings from the 1970 British Cohort Study. *Journal of Epidemiology and Community Health*, 62(5), e10–10.

Calvin, C. M., Batty, G. D., Lowe, G. and Deary, I. J. 2011. Childhood intelligence and midlife inflammatory and hemostatic biomarkers: The National Child Development Study (1958) cohort. *Health Psychology*, 30(6), 710.

Cameron, A. C. and Trivedi, P. K. 2005. *Microeconometrics: Methods and Applications*. Cambridge: Cambridge University Press.

Cameron, A. C. and Trivedi, P. K. 2009. *Microeconometrics Using Stata (Vol. 5)*. College Station, TX: Stata Press.

Carpenter, J. and Kenward, M. 2012. *Multiple Imputation and Its Application*. Chichester: John Wiley & Sons.

Chamberlain, G. 1979. *Analysis of Covariance with Qualitative Data*. Cambridge, MA, USA: National Bureau of Economic Research.

Chan, T. W. and Boliver, V. 2013. The grandparents effect in social mobility: Evidence from British birth cohort studies. *American Sociological Review*, 78(4), 662–78.

Chan, T. W. and Ermisch, J. 2015. Proximity of Couples to Parents: Influences of Gender, Labor Market, and Family. *Demography*, 52(2), 379–99.

Chan, T. W. and Halpin, B. 2002. Union dissolution in the United Kingdom. *International Journal of Sociology*, 76–93.

Chanfreau, J., Tanner, E., Callanan, M., Laing, K., Paylor, J., Skipp, A. and Todd, E. 2015. Wide disparities in take-up of school sports and activities. *Nuffield Foundation Report*, University of Newcastle.

Chatterjee, S. and Hadi, A. S. 2015. *Regression Analysis by Example*. Chichester: John Wiley & Sons.

Clark, B., Chatterjee, K., Melia, S., Knies, G. and Laurie, H. 2014. Life Events and Travel Behavior: Exploring the Interrelationship Using UK

Household Longitudinal Study Data. *Transportation Research Record: Journal of the Transportation Research Board,* 54–64.

Clark, T. S. and Linzer, D. A. 2015. Should I use fixed or random effects? *Political Science Research and Methods,* 3(02), 399–408.

Clark, W. A. and Coulter, R. 2015. Who wants to move? The role of neighbourhood change. *Environment and Planning A,* 47(12), 2683–709.

Clarke, P., Crawford, C., Steele, F. and Vignoles, A. F. 2010. *The choice between fixed and random effects models: Some considerations for educational research.* IZA Discussion Paper No. 5287.

Cleves, M. 2016. *An Introduction to Survival Analysis Using Stata.* College Station, TX: Stata Press.

Connelly, R. 2011a. Drivers of unhealthy weight in childhood: Analysis of the Millennium Cohort Study. Scottish Government Social Research.

Connelly, R. 2011b. Social stratification and cognitive ability: An assessment of the influence of childhood ability test scores and family background on occupational position across the lifespan. In: Lambert, P. S., Connelly, R., Blackburn, R. M. and Gayle, V. (eds.) *Social Stratification: Trends and Processes.* Farnham: Ashgate.

Connelly, R. and Gayle, V. 2015. Are there changing socio-economic inequalities in childhood cognitive test performance? Methodological considerations from the analysis of three British birth cohort studies. *Understanding Society Scientific Conference 2015.* University of Essex.

Connelly, R. and Platt, L. 2014. Cohort Profile: UK Millennium Cohort Study (MCS). *International Journal of Epidemiology,* 43(6), 1719–25.

Connelly, R., Gayle, V. and Lambert, P. S. 2016a. Modelling key variables in social science research: Introduction to the special section. *Methodological Innovations,* 9, 1–2.

Connelly, R., Gayle, V. and Lambert, P. S. 2016b. Statistical modelling of key variables in social survey data analysis. *Methodological Innovations,* 9, 1–17.

Connelly, R., Playford, C. J., Gayle, V. and Dibben, C. 2016c. The role of administrative data in the big data revolution in social science research. *Social Science Research,* 59, 1–12.

Cooksey, E., Joshi, H. and Verropoulou, G. 2009. Does mothers' employment affect children's development? Evidence from the children of the British 1970 Birth Cohort and the American NLSY79. *Longitudinal and Life Course Studies,* 1(1).

Cornwell, C. and Rupert, P. 1988. Efficient estimation with panel data: An empirical comparison of instrumental variables estimators. *Journal of Applied Econometrics*, 3, 149–55.

Cox, D. R. 1972. Regression models and life tables (with discussion). *Journal of the Royal Statistical Society Series B*, 34, 187–220.

Cox, D. R. and Oakes, D. 1984. *Analysis of Survival Data*. Chapman Hall/CRC, Boca Raton, FL: CRC Press.

Croxford, L. 2006. *The Youth cohort surveys: How good is the evidence?* CES Briefing, Vol. 38, Centre for Educational Sociology, University of Edinburgh.

Dale, A. and Davies, R. B. 1994. *Analyzing Social and Political Change: A Casebook of Methods*. London: Sage.

Davie, R., Butler, N. and Goldstein, H. 1972. *From Birth to Seven*. London: Longmans.

Davies, R. B. 1994. From cross-sectional to longitudinal analysis. In: Dale, A. and Davies, R. B. (eds.). *Analyzing Social and Political Change: A Casebook of Methods*, London: Sage, 20–40.

Davies, R. B., Elias, P. and Penn, R. 1992. The relationship between a husband's unemployment and his wife's participation in the labour force. *Oxford Bulletin of Economics and Statistics*, 54(2), 145–71.

Davillas, A., Benzeval, M. and Kumari, M. 2016. Association of Adiposity and Mental Health Functioning across the Lifespan: Findings from Understanding Society (The UK Household Longitudinal Study). *PLoS One*, 11(2), e0148561. https://doi.org/10.1371/journal.pone.0148561

De Vaus, D. 2013. *Surveys in Social Research*, London: Routledge.

Deary, I. J., Watson, R., Booth, T. and Gale, C. R. 2013. Does cognitive ability influence responses to the Warwick-Edinburgh Mental Well-Being Scale? *Psychological Assessment*, 25(2), 313.

Dex, S. and Joshi, H. 2006. *Children of the 21st Century: From Birth to Nine Months*. Bristol: Policy Press.

Douglas, J. W. B. 1964. *The Home and the School*. London: MacGibbon and Kee.

Douglas, J. W. B. and Blomfield, J. M. 1958. *Children under five*. London: Allen and Unwin.

Douglas, J. W. B., Ross, J. M. and Simpson, H.R. 1968. *All Our Futures: A Longitudinal Survey of Secondary Education*. London: Peter Davies.

Drew, D., Gray, J. and Sime, N. 1992. *Against the Odds: The Education and Labour Market Experiences of Black Young People*, Research Strategy Branch, Employment Department.

Ehling, M. 2003. Harmonising data in official statistics. *Advances in Cross-National Comparison*. New York, NY: Springer.

Elias, P. 2014. Administrative Data. In: Duşa, A., Nelle, D., Stock, G. and Wagner, G. (eds.) *Facing the Future: European Research Infrastructures for the Humanities and Social Sciences*. Berlin: Scivero Verlag.

Elliott, J. 2002. The value of event history techniques for understanding social processes: Modelling women's employment behaviour after motherhood. *International Journal of Social Research Methodology*, 5(2), 107–32.

Elliott, J. 2013. Talkin' 'Bout My Generation': Perceptions of Generational Belonging Among the 1958 Cohort. *Sociological Research Online*, 18(4), 13.

Elliott, J. and Shepherd, P. 2006. Cohort profile: 1970 British birth cohort (BCS70). *International Journal of Epidemiology*, 35(4), 836–43.

Ermisch, J. and Francesconi, M. 2000. Cohabitation in Great Britain: not for long, but here to stay. *Journal of the Royal Statistical Society: Series A (Statistics in Society)*, 163(2), 153–71.

Ermisch, J. and Wright, R. E. 2005. *Changing Scotland: Evidence from the British Household Panel Survey*. Bristol: Policy Press.

Ermisch, J., Gambetta, D., Laurie, H., Siedler, T. and Noah Uhrig, S. 2009. Measuring people's trust. *Journal of the Royal Statistical Society: Series A (Statistics in Society)*, 172(4), 749–69.

Exeter, D. J. 2004. *A Small Area Analysis of Mortality Inequalities in Scotland, 1980–2001*. University of St Andrews.

Fertig, A. R. 2010. Selection and the effect of prenatal smoking. *Health Economics*, 19(2), 209–26. doi:10.1002/hec.v19:2.

Fielding, A. 2004. The role of the Hausman test and whether higher level effects should be treated as random or fixed. *Multilevel Modelling Newsletter*, 16, 3–9.

Fine, J. P. and Gray, R. J. 1999. A proportional hazards model for the subdistribution of a competing risk. *Journal of the American Statistical Association*, 94, 496–509.

Firebaugh, G. 1997. *Analyzing Repeated Surveys*. Thousand Oaks, CA: Sage.

Flanagan, K. D. and West, J. 2004. Children Born in 2001: First Results from the Base Year of the Early Childhood Longitudinal Study, Birth Cohort (ECLS–B). ED TAB. NCES 2005-036. *US Department of Education*.

Fotouhi, A. R. 1990. *Longitudinal data analysis: The initial conditions problem in random effects modelling*. PhD, Lancaster University.

Fotouhi, A. R. and Davies, R. B. 2007. The initial conditions problem in modelling repeated durations: A simulation study. *Simulation Modelling Practice and Theory*, 15(9), 1120–27.

Frick, J. R., Jenkins, S. P., Lillard, D. R., Lipps, O. and Wooden, M. 2007. The Cross-National Equivalent File (CNEF) and its member country household panel studies. *Schmollers Jahrbuch: Zeitschrift für Wirtschafts-und Sozialwissenschaften*, 127(4), 627–54.

Furstenberg, F. F. and Kiernan, K. E. 2001. Delayed parental divorce: How much do children benefit? *Journal of Marriage and Family*, 63(2), 446–57.

Ganzeboom, H. B., Luijkx, R. and Treiman, D. J. 1989. Intergenerational class mobility in comparative perspective. *Research in social Stratification and Mobility*, 8, 3–79.

Gayle, V. 2005. Youth transitions. In: Ermisch, J. and Wright, R.E. eds., *Changing Scotland: Evidence from the British Household Panel Survey*, Bristol: Policy Press, 77–98.

Gayle, V. and Lambert, P. 2017. The Workflow: A Practical Guide to Producing Accurate, Efficient, Transparent and Reproducible Social Survey Data Analysis. National Centre for Research Methods, Working Paper 1/17.

Gayle, V., Murray, S. and Connelly, R. 2016. Young people and school General Certificate of Secondary Education attainment: Looking for the 'missing middle'. *British Journal of Sociology of Education*, 37(3), 350–70.

Gehan, E. A. 1965. A generalized Wilcoxon test for comparing arbitrarily singly-censored samples. *Biometrika*, 52(1–2), 203–23.

Gelman, A. 2005. Analysis of variance—why it is more important than ever. *The Annals of Statistics*, 33(1), 1–53.

Gelman, A. and Hill, J. 2007. *Data Analysis Using Regression and Multilevel Hierarchical Models*. Cambridge: Cambridge University Press.

Glenn, N. D. 1974. Aging and conservatism. *The ANNALS of the American Academy of Political and Social Science*, 415(1), 176–86.

Glenn, N. D. 1976. Cohort analysts' futile quest: Statistical attempts to separate age, period and cohort effects. *American Sociological Review*, 41(5), 900–4.

Goldring, S. and Newman, J. 2010. The ONS Longitudinal Study-a prestigious past and a bright future. *Population Trends*, 139(1), 4–10.

Goldstein, H. 1999. *Multilevel Statistical Models*. London: Arnold.

Goldstein, H. 2011. *Multilevel Statistical Models*. Chichester: John Wiley & Sons.

Goldstein, H., Browne, W. and Rasbash, J. 2002. Partitioning variation in multilevel models. *Understanding Statistics: Statistical Issues in Psychology, Education, and the Social Sciences*, 1(4), 223–31.

Goldthorpe, J. H. and Mills, C. 2008. Trends in intergenerational class mobility in modern Britain: Evidence from national surveys, 1972–2005. *National Institute Economic Review*, 205(1), 83–100.

Grambsch, P. M. and Therneau, T. M. 1994. Proportional hazards tests and diagnostics based on weighted residuals. *Biometrika*, 81(3), 515–526.

Gray, M. and Sanson, A. 2005. Growing up in Australia: The longitudinal study of Australian children. *Family Matters*, (72), 4–9.

Green, M.. 2016. Do the companionship and community networks of older LGBT adults compensate for weaker kinship networks? *Quality in Ageing and Older Adults*, 17(1), 36–49. https://doi.org/10.1108/QAOA-07-2015-0032

Greene, W. H. 1999. *Econometric Analysis*. Harlow: Pearson Education.

Greene, W. H. 2012a. *Econometric Analysis*. 7th edn. Upper Saddle River, NJ: Prentice Hall.

Greene, W. H. and Hensher, D. A. 2010. *Modeling Ordered Choices: A Primer*. Cambridge: Cambridge University Press.

Gregg, P. and Tominey, E. 2005. The wage scar from male youth unemployment. *Labour Economics*, 12(4), 487–509.

Hadjar, A. and Samuel, R. 2015. Does upward social mobility increase life satisfaction? A longitudinal analysis using British and Swiss panel data. *Research in Social Stratification and Mobility*, 39, 48–58.

Halaby, C. N. 2004. Panel models in sociological research: Theory into practice. *Annual Review of Sociology*, 30, 507–44.

Hamilton, L. 2012. *Statistics with Stata: Version 12*. Boston, MA: Brooks/Cole, Cengage Learning.

Hansen, K. 2014. Millennium Cohort Study A Guide to the Datasets (Eighth Edition) First, Second, Third, Fourth and Fifth Surveys. Institute of Education, University of London.

Hansen, K., Joshi, H. and Dex, S. 2010. *Children of the 21st Century: The First Five Years*. Bristol: Policy Press.

Harford, T. 2014. Big data: A big mistake? *Significance*, 11(5), 14–19.

Harkness, J. A., Van De Vijver, F. J. and Mohler, P. P. 2003. *Cross-Cultural Survey Methods*. Hoboken, NJ: Wiley-Interscience.

Harkness, J. A., De Leeuw, E. D., Hox, J. J. and Dillman, D. A. 2008. *International Handbook of Survey Methodology.* NJ: Lawrence Erlbaum.

Harper, S. 2015. Invited commentary: APC... It's easy as 1-2-3! *American Journal of Epidemiology*, 182(4), 313–7.

Hausman, J. A. 1978. Specification tests in econometrics. *Econometrica*, 46(6), 1251–71.

Heckman, J. J. 2001. Micro data, heterogeneity, and the evaluation of public policy: Nobel lecture. *Journal of Political Economy*, 109, 673–48.

Heckman, J. J. and Borjas, G. J. 1980. Does unemployment cause future unemployment? Definitions, questions and answers from a continuous time model of heterogeneity and state dependence. *Economica*, 47(187), 247–83.

Hedeker, D. 2005. Generalized linear mixed models. In: Everitt, B. and Howell, D. (eds.) *Encyclopaedia of Statistics in Behavioral Science.* New York: Wiley.

Hedeker, D. and Gibbons, R. D. 2006. *Longitudinal Data Analysis.* Hoboken, NJ: John Wiley & Sons.

Henley, A. 1998. Residential mobility, housing equity and the labour market. *The Economic Journal*, 108(447), 414–27.

Hill, M. S. 1992. *The Panel Study of Income Dynamics: A users guide.* Newbury Park, CA: Sage Publications.

Hobcraft, J. and Sacker, A. 2011. Guest editorial: The origins of Understanding Society. *Longitudinal and Life Course Studies*, 3(1), 1–4.

Hoffmeyer-Zlotnik, J. H. and Warner, U. 2014. *Harmonising Demographic and Socio-Economic Variables for Cross-National Comparative Survey Research.* Dordrecht: Springer Science & Business Media.

Hox, J. J., Moerbeek, M. and Van De Schoot, R. 2010. *Multilevel Analysis: Techniques and Applications.* Hove: Routledge.

Hsiao, C. 2014. *Analysis of Panel Data.* New York, NY: Cambridge University Press.

Huber, P. J. 1967. The behavior of maximum likelihood estimates under nonstandard conditions. In: Proceedings of the fifth Berkeley symposium on mathematical statistics and probability, 1(1), 221–33.

Jaszczak, A., Lundeen, K. and Smith, S. 2009. Using nonmedically trained interviewers to collect biomeasures in a national in-home survey. *Field Methods*, 21(1), 26–48.

Jenkins, S. P. 2000. Modelling household income dynamics. *Journal of Population Economics*, 13(4), 529–67.

Jerrim, J., Vignoles, A., Lingam, R. and Friend, A. 2015. The socio-economic gradient in children's reading skills and the role of genetics. *British Educational Research Journal*, 41(1), 6–29.

Johnson, T. P. 1998. Approaches to equivalence in cross-cultural and cross-national survey research. In: Harkness, J. (ed.), *Zentrum für Umfragen, Methoden und Analysen -ZUMA- (Ed.): Cross-cultural survey equivalence.* Mannheim, 1–40 (ZUMA-Nachrichten Spezial 3). ISBN 3-924220-13-1. URN: http://nbn-resolving.de/ urn:nbn:de:0168-ssoar-49730-6.

Jowell, R., Roberts, C., Fitzgerald, R. and Eva, G. 2007. *Measuring Attitudes Cross-Nationally: Lessons from the European Social Survey.* London: Sage.

Kaiser, A. 2013. A Review of Longitudinal Datasets on Ageing. *Journal of Population Ageing*, 6(1–2), 5–27.

Kelly, Y., Panico, L., Bartley, M., Marmot, M., Nazroo, J. and Sacker, A. 2009. Why does birthweight vary among ethnic groups in the UK? Findings from the Millennium Cohort Study. *Journal of Public Health*, 31(1), 131–7.

Ketende, S. and Jones, E. 2011a. *The Millennium Cohort Study: User Guide to Analysing MCS Data Using STATA.* London: Centre for Longitudinal Studies Institute of Education.

Ketende, S. and Jones, E. 2011b. *User Guide to Analysing MCS Data Using Stata.* Centre for Longitudinal Studies.

Kiernan, K. and Mueller, G. 1998. The divorced and who divorces? London: London School of Economics.

Knies, G. 2014. *Understanding Society–UK household longitudinal study: Wave 1–4, 2009–2013,* user manual. Colchester: University of Essex.

Kohler, H. P. and Kreuter, F. 2012. *Data Analysis Using Stata.* College Station, Tx: Stata Press.

Kuh, D., Cooper, R., Hardy, R., Richards, M. and Ben-Shlomo, Y. (eds.) 2013. *A Life Course Approach to Healthy Ageing.* Oxford: OUP Oxford.

Lambert, P., Prandy, K. and Bottero, W. 2007. By slow degrees: Two centuries of social reproduction and mobility in Britain. *Sociological Research Online*, 12(1).

Laurie, H. M. and Wright, R. E. 2000. The Scottish household panel survey. *Scottish Journal of Political Economy*, 47(3), 337–9.

Lazarsfeld, P. and Fiske, M. 1938. The "panel" as a new tool for measuring opinion. *The Public Opinion Quarterly*, 2(4), 596–612.

Lee, E. T. and Wang, J. 2003. *Statistical Methods for Survival Data Analysis*. Hoboken, NJ: John Wiley & Sons.

Liao, T. F. 1994. *Interpreting Probability Models: Logit, Probit, and Other Generalized Linear Models*. London: Sage.

Lillard, D. R. and Burkhauser, R. V. 2006. Evaluation of the Cross-National Comparability of the Survey of Health, Ageing, and Retirement in Europe, the Health and Retirement Study, and the English Longitudinal Study of Ageing. Report prepared for the National Institutes of Aging, Washington, DC.

Lillard, L. A., Brien, M. J. and Waite, L. J. 1995. Premarital cohabitation and subsequent marital. *Demography*, 32(3), 437–57.

Long, J. S. 2009. *The Workflow of Data Analysis Using Stata*. College Station, TX: Stata Press, 379.

Long, J. S. and Freese, J. 2014. *Regression Models for Categorical Dependent Variables Using Stata*. College Station, TX: Stata press.

Longhi, S. and Nandi, A. 2014. *A Practical Guide to Using Panel Data*. London: Sage.

Lynn, P. 2009a. *Methodology of Longitudinal Surveys*. Hoboken, NJ: John Wiley & Sons.

Lynn, P. 2009b. Sample design for understanding society. Understanding Society, Understanding Society Working Paper 2009-01, No. 2009-01, Colchester: ISER, University of Essex.

Lynn, P. and Kaminska, O. 2010. Weighting strategy for Understanding Society. Working Paper No. 2010-05, Colchester: ISER, University of Essex.

Mantel, N. and Haenszel, W. 1959. Statistical aspects of the analysis of data from retrospective studies. *Journal of the National Cancer Institute*, 22(4), 719–48.

Marmot, M. 2004. Status syndrome. *Significance*, 1(4), 150–4.

Marmot, M. and Brunner, E. 2005. Cohort profile: The Whitehall II study. *International Journal of Epidemiology*, 34(2), 251–6.

Mayer, K. U. and Svallfors, S. 2005. Life courses and life chances in a comparative perspective. *Analyzing Inequality: Life Chances and Social Mobility in Comparative Perspective*, 17–55.

Mcaloney, K., Graham, H., Law, C., Platt, L. and Wardle, H. 2014. Inter-generational concordance of smoking status between mothers and young people aged 10–15 in the UK. *Public Health*, 128(9), 831–3.

Mcfadden, D. 1973. Conditional logit analysis of qualitative choice behavior. In: Zarembka, P. (ed.) *Frontiers in Econometrics*. New York: Academic Press.

Mcfall, S. L., Conolly, A. and Burton, J. 2014. Collecting biomarkers using trained interviewers. Lessons learned from a pilot study. *Survey research methods*, 8(1), 57–66.

Mcfall, S. L., Booker, C., Burton, J. and Conolly, A. 2012. Implementing the biosocial component of Understanding Society–nurse collection of biomeasures. Understanding Society Working Paper Series No. 2012 – 04 ISER, University of Essex.

Mcginnis, R. 1968. A stochastic model of social mobility. *American Sociological Review*, 33(5), 712–22.

Mehmetoglu, M. and Jakobsen, T. G. 2016. *Applied Statistics Using Stata: A Guide for the Social Sciences*. London: Sage.

Melotti, R., Heron, J., Hickman, M., Macleod, J., Araya, R. and Lewis, G. 2011. Adolescent alcohol and tobacco use and early socioeconomic position: The ALSPAC birth cohort. *Pediatrics*, 127, e948–955.

Menard, S. 1995. *Applied logistic regression analysis: Sage university series on quantitative applications in the social sciences*. Thousand Oaks, CA: Sage.

Mitchell, M. N. 2010. *Data Management Using Stata: A Practical Handbook*. College Station, TX: Stata Press.

Mitchell, M. N. and Chen, X. 2005. Visualizing main effects and interactions for binary logit models. *Stata Journal*, 5(1), 64–82.

Mokrysz, C., Landy, R., Gage, S., Munafò, M., Roiser, J. and Curran, H. 2016. Are IQ and educational outcomes in teenagers related to their cannabis use? A prospective cohort study. *Journal of Psychopharmacology*, 30(2), 159–168.

Morton, S. M., Carr, P. E. A., Grant, C. C., Robinson, E. M., Bandara, D. K., Bird, A., Ivory, V. C., Te Kani, R. K., Liang, R. and Marks, E. J. 2013. Cohort profile: Growing up in New Zealand. *International Journal of Epidemiology*, 42(1), 65–75.

Moser, C. A. and Kalton, G. 1971. *Survey Methods in Social Investigation*. London: Ashgate Publishing.

MRC 2014. *Maximising the Value of the UK Populations Cohorts*. Swindon: Medical Research Council.

Mulder, C. H. and Smits, J. 1999. First-time home-ownership of couples the effect of inter-generational transmission. *European Sociological Review*, 15(3), 323–37.

Mundlak, Y. 1978. On the pooling of time series and cross section data. *Econometrica: Journal of the Econometric Society*, 46(1), 69–85.

Nelder, J. A. and Wedderburn, R. W. M. 1972. Generalized Linear Models. *Journal of the Royal Statistical Society: Series A (General)*, 135(3), 370–84.

Nickell, S. 1981. Biases in dynamic models with fixed effects. *Econometrica: Journal of the Econometric Society*, 1417–26.

Norton, E. C., Wang, H. and Ai, C. 2004. Computing interaction effects and standard errors in logit and probit models. *Stata Journal*, 4, 154–67.

Nowok, B., Van Ham, M., Findlay, A. M. and Gayle, V. 2013. Does migration make you happy? A longitudinal study of internal migration and subjective well-being. *Environment and Planning A*, 45(4), 986–1002.

O'Reilly, D., Rosato, M., Maguire, A. and Wright, D. 2015. Caregiving reduces mortality risk for most caregivers: A census-based record linkage study. *International Journal of Epidemiology*, 44(6), 1959–69.

O'Reilly, D., Rosato, M., Catney, G., Johnston, F. and Brolly, M. 2012. Cohort description: The Northern Ireland Longitudinal Study (NILS). *International Journal of Epidemiology*, 41(3), 634–41.

Parkes, A., Sweeting, H. and Wight, D. 2014. Growing Up in Scotland: Family and school influences on children's social and emotional well-being. Edinburgh: Scottish Government.

Parkes, A., Sweeting, H. and Wight, D. 2015. Parenting stress and parent support among mothers with high and low education. *Journal of Family Psychology*, 29(6), 907–18.

Parkes, A., Sweeting, H. and Wight, D. 2016. Early Childhood Precursors and School age Correlates of Different Internalising Problem Trajectories Among Young Children. *Journal of Abnormal Child Psychology*, 44(7), 1333–346.

Pearson, H. 2016. *The Life Project: The Extraordinary Story of 70,000 Ordinary Lives*. London: Penguin Books.

Persson, I. 2002. Essays on the Assumption of Proportional Hazards in Cox Regression (Doctoral dissertation, Acta Universitatis Upsaliensis).

Pevalin, D. J. and Ermisch, J. 2004. Cohabiting unions, repartnering and mental health. *Psychological Medicine*, 34(08), 1553–59.

Pevalin, D. J. and Robson, K. 2009. *The Stata Survival Manual*. Maidenhead, UK: McGraw-Hill Education.

Platt, L., Simpson, L. and Akinwale, B. 2005. Stability and change in ethnic groups in England and Wales. *Population Trends-London*, 121, 35–46.

Platt, L., Smith, K., Parsons, S., Connelly, R., Joshi, H., Rosenberg, R., Hansen, K., Brown, M., Sullivan, A., Chatzitheochari, S. and Mostafa, T. 2014. *Millennium Cohort Study: Initial Findings from the Age 11 Survey*. London: Centre for Longitudinal Studies, Institute of Education.

Playford, C. J. and Gayle, V. 2016. The concealed middle? An exploration of ordinary young people and school GCSE subject area attainment. *Journal of Youth Studies*, 19(2), 149–68.

Playford, C. J., Gayle, V., Connelly, R. and Gray, A. J. 2016. Administrative social science data: The challenge of reproducible research. *Big Data & Society*, 3(2), 1–10.

Plewis, I. 1997. *Statistics in Education*. London: Arnold.

Plewis, I., Calderwood, L., Hawkes, D., Hughes, G. and Joshi, H. 2007. *Millennium Cohort Study: Technical Report on Sampling*. London: Centre for Longitudinal Study, Institute of Education.

Power, C. and Elliott, J. 2006. Cohort profile: 1958 British birth cohort (national child development study). *International Journal of Epidemiology*, 35(1), 34–41.

Prandy, K. 1990. The revised Cambridge scale of occupations. *Sociology*, 24(4), 629–55.

Quigley, M. A., Kelly, Y. J. and Sacker, A. 2007. Breastfeeding and hospitalization for diarrheal and respiratory infection in the United Kingdom Millennium Cohort Study. *Pediatrics*, 119(4), e837–42.

Rabe, B. 2011. Geographical identifiers in Understanding Society Version 1. Understanding Society Working Paper Series 2011-01, Institute of Social and Economic Research, University of Essex.

Rabe-Hesketh, S. and Skrondal, A. 2012. *Multilevel and Longitudinal Modeling Using Stata (third edition)*. College Station, TX: Stata Press.

Rabe-Hesketh, S., Skrondal, A. and Pickles, A. 2004. GLLAMM Manual. U.C. Berkeley Division of Biostatistics Working Paper Series. Working Paper 160.

Rafferty, A., Walthery, P. and King-Hele, S. 2015. *Analysing change over time: Repeated cross-sectional and longitudinal survey data.* UK Data Service, University of Essex and University of Manchester.

Ralston, K., Gayle, V. and Lambert, P. 2016. Gender, occupation and first birth: Do career men delay first birth too? *Sociological Research Online,* 21(1), paper 3.

Raudenbush, S. W. and Bryk, A. S. 2002. *Hierarchical Linear Models: Applications and Data Analysis Methods.* Thousand Oaks, CA: Sage.

Read, S. and Grundy, E. 2012. Allostatic load and health in the older population of England: a crossed-lagged analysis. *Psychosomatic Medicine,* 76(7), 490–96.

Reid, N. 1994. A conversation with Sir David Cox. *Statistical Science,* 9, 439–55.

Rogers, W. 1994. Regression standard errors in clustered samples. *Stata Technical Bulletin,* 3(13).

Rose, D., Pevalin, D. J. and O'reilly, K. 2005. *The National Statistics Socio-economic Classification: Origins, Development and Use.* Basingstoke: Palgrave Macmillan.

Royston, P. and Lambert, P. C. 2011. *Flexible parametric survival analysis using Stata: Beyond the Cox model.* College Station, TX: Stata Press.

Sabates, R. and Dex, S. 2015. The impact of multiple risk factors on young children's cognitive and behavioural development. *Children & Society,* 29(2), 95–108.

Sala, E., Burton, J. and Knies, G. 2012. Correlates of obtaining informed consent to data linkage respondent, interview, and interviewer characteristics. *Sociological Methods and Research,* 41(3), 414–39.

Schmied, V. and Lupton, D. 2001. Blurring the boundaries: Breastfeeding and maternal subjectivity. *Sociology of Health & Illness,* 23(2), 234–50.

Searle, S., Casella, G. and McCulloch, C. 1992. *Variance Components.* Hoboken, NJ: John Wiley & Sons.

Singer, J. D. and Willett, J. B. 2003. *Applied Longitudinal Data Analysis: Modeling Change and Event Occurrence.* Oxford: Oxford University Press.

Skafida, V. and Treanor, M. C. 2014. Do changes in objective and subjective family income predict change in children's diets over time? Unique insights using a longitudinal cohort study and fixed effects analysis. *Journal of Epidemiology and Community Health,* 68(6), 534–41.

Skinner, C. J., Holt, D. and Smith, T. F. 1989. *Analysis of Complex Surveys*. Chichester, UK: John Wiley & Sons, 328.

Skrondal, A. and Rabe-Hesketh, S. 2004. *Generalized Latent Variable Modeling: Multilevel, Longitudinal, and Structural Equation Models*. Boca Raton, FL: CRC Press.

Smeeding, T. M., Jesuit, D. K. and Alkemade, P. 2002. The LIS/LES Project Databank: Introduction and Overview. *Schmollers Jahrbuch*, 122(3), 497–517.

Smith, K. and Joshi, H. 2002. The millennium cohort study. *Population Trends-London*, 107, 30–34.

Steele, F., Goldstein, H. and Browne, W. 2004. A general multilevel multistate competing risks model for event history data, with an application to a study of contraceptive use dynamics. *Statistical Modelling*, 4(2), 145–59.

Stenberg, S.-Å. and Vågerö, D. 2006. Cohort profile: The Stockholm birth cohort of 1953. *International Journal of Epidemiology*, 35(3), 546–8.

Steptoe, A., Breeze, E., Banks, J. and Nazroo, J. 2013. Cohort profile: The English longitudinal study of ageing. *International Journal of Epidemiology*, 42(6), 1640–8.

Stewart, M. B. 2006. Maximum simulated likelihood estimation of random-effects dynamic probit models with autocorrelated errors. *Stata Journal*, 6(2), 256–72.

Stewart, M. B. 2007. The interrelated dynamics of unemployment and low-wage employment. *Journal of Applied Econometrics*, 22(3), 511–31.

Stewart-Brown, S. and Haslum, M. 1988. Partial sight and blindness in children of the 1970 birth cohort at 10 years of age. *Journal of Epidemiology and Community Health*, 42(1), 17–23.

Suárez, E. L., Pérez, C. M., Nogueras, G. M. and Moreno-Gorrín, C. 2016. *Biostatistics in Public Health Using STATA*. Boca Raton, FL: CRC Press.

Tanner, E., Chanfreau, J., Challanan, M., Laing, K., Paylor, J., Skipp, A., Todd, L. 2016. Can out of school activities close the education gap? Briefing paper 4. London: NatCen Social Research. Out of school activities & the education gap 4.

Taris, T. W. 2000. *A Primer in Longitudinal Data Analysis*. London: Sage.

Taylor, M. F., Brice, J., Buck, N. and Prentice-Lane, E. 1996. *British Household Panel Survey User Manual*. Colchester: ESRC Research Centre on Micro-social Change, University of Essex.

Taylor, M. F., Brice, J., Buck, N. and Prentice-Lane, E. 2010. *British Household Panel Survey User Manual Volume A: Introduction, Technical Report and Appendices.* Colchester: University of Essex.

Therneau, T. M. 1997. Extending the Cox model. In: Lin, D.Y., Fleming T.R. (eds) Proceedings of the First Seattle Symposium in Biostatistics. Lecture Notes in Statistics, Vol. 123. New York, NY: Springer, 51–84.

Treiman, D. J. 2009. *Quantitative Data Analysis: Doing Social Research to Test Ideas.* San Francisco: John Wiley & Sons.

Tuma, N. B. 1982. Nonparametric and partially parametric approaches to event-history analysis. *Sociological Methodology*, 13, 1–60.

Turner, S., Alborz, A. and Gayle, V. 2008. Predictors of academic attainments of young people with Down's syndrome. *Journal of Intellectual Disability Research*, 52(5), 380–92.

Uhrig, S. N. 2011. Using experiments to guide decision making in Understanding Society: Introducing the Innovation Panel. In McFall, S. L. and Garrington, C. (eds.). *Understanding Society: Early findings from the first wave of the UK's household longitudinal study, Institute for Social and Economic Research.* Colchester: University of Essex.

Van Deth, J. W. 2003. *Using Published Survey Data.* Chichester: Wiley, 291–307.

Viner, R. M. and Taylor, B. 2007. Adult outcomes of binge drinking in adolescence: Findings from a UK national birth cohort. *Journal of Epidemiology and Community Health*, 61(10), 902–7.

Wadsworth, M., Kuh, D., Richards, M. and Hardy, R. 2006. Cohort profile: The 1946 national birth cohort (MRC National Survey of Health and Development). *International Journal of Epidemiology*, 35(1), 49–54.

Wagner, G. G., Burkhauser, R.V. and Behringer, F. 1993. The English language public use file of the German Socio-Economic Panel. *Journal of Human resources*, 28, 429–33.

Webber, M. 1994. Survey of labour and income dynamics: an overview. In Report 1994, Cat. 75-201E. Ottawa: Statistics Canada.

Weinstein, M., Vaupel, J. W. and Wachter, K. W. 2007. *Biosocial Surveys.* Washington, DC: National Academies Press.

Welsh Language Unit 2012. *A living language: A language for living (Welsh Language Strategy 2012–17).* Welsh Assembly.

White, H. 1984. *Asymptotic Theory for Econometricians.* Academic Press.

Willett, J. B. and Singer, J. D. 1995. It's déjà vu all over again: Using multiple-spell discrete-time survival analysis. *Journal of Educational and Behavioral Statistics*, 20(1), 41–67.

Wooden, M., Freidin, S. and Watson, N. 2002. The household, income and labour dynamics in Australia (HILDA) survey: Wave 1. *Australian Economic Review*, 35(3), 339–48.

Wooldridge, J. M. 2005. Fixed-effects and related estimators for correlated random-coefficient and treatment-effect panel data models. *Review of Economics and Statistics*, 87(2), 385–90.

Wooldridge, J. M. 2010. *Econometric Analysis of Cross Section and Panel Data*. Cambridge, MA: MIT press.

Yang, Y. and Land, K. C. 2008. Age–period–cohort analysis of repeated cross-section surveys: Fixed or random effects? *Sociological Methods and Research*, 36(3), 297–326.

Zorn, C. J. 2000. Modeling duration dependence. *Political Analysis*, 367–80.

Zwysen, W. 2015. The effects of father's worklessness on young adults in the UK. *IZA Journal of European Labor Studies*, 4(2), 1–15.

Index